F

KEVIN RANDLE and RUSS ESTES

A FIRESIDE BOOK/ Published by Simon & Schuster

FACES OF THE VISITORS

An Illustrated Reference to Alien Contact

F

FIRESIDE
Rockefeller Center
1230 Avenue of the Americas
New York, NY 10020

FIRESIDE and colophon are registered trademarks
of Simon & Schuster Inc.

Manufactured in the United States of America

1   2   3   4   5   6   7   8   9   10

Library of Congress Cataloging-in-Publication Data

Randle, Kevin D., date.
Faces of the visitors : an illustrated reference to alien contact /
[Kevin Randle and Russ Estes].
p.   cm.
Includes bibliographical references and index.
1. Human–alien encounters—Case studies.   2. Life on other
planets—Case studies.   3. Alien abduction—Case studies.
I. Estes, Russ.   II. Title.
BF2050.R35   1997
001.942—dc21   97-30932
CIP

ISBN 0-684-83973-3

Acknowledgments

Thanks to all the UFO researchers who have contributed their work to a field that has been ignored by both the journalistic and scientific communities. Without their untiring and often unrewarded work, we would all be poorer. Thanks also to the brave souls who have told their tales of alien contact in spite of the ridicule often directed at them for speaking out. And finally thanks to those who have published all the material so that we could learn the truth.

A special thank-you to Antonio Huneeus for kindly allowing us to use his information about some of the foreign cases he has investigated. And special thanks to Timothy Green Beckley, editor of *UFO Universe* and the driving force behind Global Communications, for his kindness in allowing us to use his photographs.

Author's Note: We have attempted to keep the illustrations as close as possible to those originally offered by witnesses. Russ Estes did a great deal of work on each illustration in our attempt to make them as accurate as possible. We have attempted to contact the various copyright holders to secure the proper permissions. If we have missed anyone, it is accidental.

Contents

Introduction

Abduction researchers once thought that 85 percent of alien creatures reported could be characterized as grays—creatures smaller than humans with inverted teardrop-shaped heads and large almond-shaped black eyes. As we compiled this book, however, we found that the alien creatures reported since June 1947 were anything but standardized. Literally hundreds of types of creatures had been reported by thousands of different witnesses in many parts of the world.

In compiling this work, we used hundreds of different sources, ranging from the original reports of the witnesses to the books and magazines that have appeared in the last fifty years. We have tried to suggest the appearance of the creatures by making our work conform as closely as possible to the original drawings and descriptions provided by the witnesses. We used the records compiled for Project Blue Book, the official U.S. Air Force investigation. We were also able to use the records compiled by now defunct civilian investigations including those by the National Investigations Committee on Aerial Phenomena (NICAP) and the Aerial Phenomena Research Organization (APRO).

It has been suggested by skeptics and critics that our idea of what the visitors look like, though once heavily influenced by ancient myths and legends, is now influenced by movies and books.

Close Encounters of the Third Kind, the spectacular 1977 movie, for example, is said to have contributed greatly to our current image of alien visitors.

Some of the most commonly reported "uniforms" worn by aliens in the early days were "diving suits" like the ones shown in countless science-fiction films. People who reported alien beings early on seemed to believe the visitors would be unable to breathe in our atmosphere and so would require a self-contained environment. According to *Flying Saucer Occupants* by Coral and Jim Lorenzen, many of those early reports, especially from France and South America, mentioned beings in diving suits.

Later, as the contactee phenomenon began to spread and movies were made showing other planets with Earth-type atmospheres, the diving suits gave way to silver jumpsuits. People seem to have been reporting what they expected to see based on what they had seen in the movies and on television or what they had read about in books.

In a survey of the literature, then, we see a diversity of UFO occupants in the early years, which persisted until the media influence became overwhelming. Once *Star Trek* suggested that Earthlike planets existed throughout the galaxy, the stories of little men in space suits gave way to other descriptions. There is little doubt that the media have influenced the descriptions of aliens.

We are not suggesting that all of the reports were invented or, on the other hand, that all of them are true. These tales are what the witnesses themselves have reported to the air force or to the civilian UFO organizations. Those witnesses may have been influenced by pop culture, by television and movies, by the reports of others, or by their own imaginations. Or they may not have been influenced by anything other than what they really did see during their encounters.

We have gathered what we consider to be a representative sample of the alien beings reported. Some of them look amazingly human; these beings are sometimes known as Nordics. Others, of course, are the little gray creatures that have graced so many tales of alien abduction. And still others are impossibly grotesque beasts that resemble nothing intelligent yet seem to have the capability to build spacecraft and traverse vast interstellar distances.

We have attempted to tell the story of each encounter in sufficient detail that the reader can make an intelligent decision about the validity of the report. Yes, some of them are so far out that they are impossible to believe. There are claims by both contactees and abductees, for example, of riding in the saucers to the home worlds of the alien pilots. There are suggestions of impressive physical evidence that somehow always eludes us. We have also provided a variety of sources where additional information or contrary views can be found.

In an attempt to provide the reader with an idea, in our professional estimation, of how reliable each encounter is, we have given each one a reliability rating. It ranges from zero, which means no reliability, to ten, which means there was actual proof that an alien had been seen. The highest rating we give is a nine, and that is because of the number of witnesses who reported the sighting, their credibility, and their standing in the community or their official positions with the government.

You may notice along the way that some truly incredible cases are given fairly high ratings. The reason for this is that a number of witnesses were involved in those specific events. If a dozen people reported the same thing and corroborated the tale told by the others, no matter how outlandish, we have given it a high reliablity rating.

On the other hand, we gave low numbers to some cases that are universally accepted. Again, it is because of the lack of good corroboration. The number and the credibility of the witnesses were our main criteria in determining an encounter's rating. It should be noted, of course, that the reliability rating is our subjective opinion. We are aware that we tend to favor some unbelievable stories over others that are just as unbelievable. This results from a combination of our extensive work in the field and just how wild some of the tales have become.

A wide variety of alien encounters have been reported around the world over the years, but for this book we have broken them down into three main categories. Some we call close encounters of the third kind (CE-III), meaning the witness saw the alien at close range, may have interacted with it in some fashion, or maybe just glimpsed it. Reports of these types of encounters fill Part I of this book. Part II comprises the tales told by *contactees,* who describe their interactions with beings who have come to help us. The third and final group is made up of *abductees,* whose stories are told in Part III. These people have reported close encounters of the fourth kind (CE-IV)—that is, they claim to have been taken aboard flying saucers—against their will, for the most part—for examination and experimentation.

So here are the aliens who reportedly have visited us. Here are the stories of those visits, based on the testimony of those who witnessed them. Here is the best analysis we can make of those tales so that you will have a sense of what may be true and accurate and what is probably a hoax or a misdirection. And finally, here are the sources of those tales so that you can check them for yourself.

4

Part I

The Visitors:
Close Encounters
of the Third Kind

Earth has been visited by alien creatures from the beginning of time. There were gods and demons, and there were fairies and gnomes, all of which can be considered alien. The ancient Romans and Greeks told epic tales of gods who lived away from the human race on Mount Olympus and descended from the heavens. These gods, of course, possessed powers of which we could only dream. They might be considered the extraterrestrial creatures of that long-ago age.

In France in 1645 a young girl named Ann Jeffries was found lying on the floor in her room in a semiconscious state, apparently suffering from a convulsion. Later she recalled being paralyzed and surrounded by six little men who covered her with kisses. After that event, she reported further contact with the "fairies." In 1646 she was arrested for witchcraft and imprisoned. It could be said that her fable was one of extraterrestrial contact, not at all unlike the reports of today.

Today's science has shown that fairies don't exist, the underworld is a myth, and modern witches practice the craft as a religion but have no magical or supernatural powers. What then should we make of the recent reports of sightings of UFOs and alien creatures in our era? Are they our versions of the myths and legends of old, or are they something new and based in reality?

We can start to explore this question by examining the stories of alien creatures that have been reported over the last fifty years. There have been hundreds of these reports of close encounters of the third kind, or CE-IIIs, and the descriptions provided are not unlike those given by our ancestors.

Like the Greeks and Romans before us, we are being told of perfect beings who descended from the heavens to offer us insight into the operation of the universe and ways to repair our damaged planet. The descriptions, from the beginning of the modern UFO era, have been limited only by the imagination of the witnesses.

The term "close encounters" was coined by former air force consultant and Northwestern University astronomy professor Dr. J. Allen Hynek. To him a close encounter of the *first* kind (CE-I) was a sighting of a craft within a hundred yards or so. A close encounter of the *second* kind (CE-II) meant that the craft had landed near the witness. And a close encounter of the *third* kind (CE-III) meant that the witness had seen the occupants of the craft.

CE-III cases provide some of the few instances in which physical evidence has been recovered. One such case was reported by police officer Lonnie Zamora.

In April 1964, while chasing a speeder, Zamora heard a detonation that he believed to be a dynamite storage shed exploding on the outskirts of Socorro, New Mexico. He drove immediately to that location and, as he slowed, saw what he thought was an overturned car. When Zamora stopped his cruiser and got out, he saw two small creatures near the object, which was egg-shaped. When they saw him, they scrambled inside their craft, and moments later it lifted off with a roar. Left behind were a burning bush and impressions of the landing gear.

This is one of the few cases in which an alien object interacted with the environment to create physical evidence. Unfortunately, however, people were so busy arguing about the authenticity of the sighting that a thorough and scientific evaluation of the evidence was not conducted.

THE VISITORS

7

The Zamora case demonstrates the problems with all UFO sightings. Here was the opportunity to find a few answers, to provide the physical evidence demanded by science; instead, science was ignored and an opportunity for valuable, reliable research was lost.

Because this kind of contention occurs in many instances, little evidence remains of most sightings beyond the testimony of the witnesses. A majority of these witnesses are sincere, honest people who have seen something that they can't adequately explain. Given the nature of the reports, we can't explain the encounters either. Without physical evidence we can't prove that the tales have been accurately reported no matter how honest and sincere the witness seems to be.

So we will now look at the visitors as they have been reported by the witnesses. We leave it up to each of you to make up your mind for yourself.

Peru:

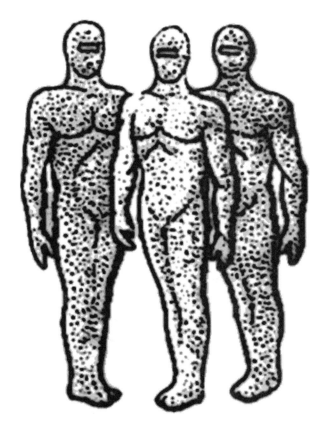

Location: Six miles south of Lima, Peru

Witnesses: C.A.V.

Encounter Type: CE-III

Craft Type: Disc

Alien Type: Humanoid

Alien Characteristics: The witness described the aliens as looking like mummies. They had a profile like that of a human, but their legs were fused together. Their hands looked like fingers in mittens, and they had an opposable thumb. The skin was sand-colored, and they had no facial features. There was a transparent area where the eyes should have been. See also the Hickson-Parker Case, October 12, 1973, in Part III (page 154).

Home World: Unknown

Sources: *UFOs over the Americas* and *Encounters with UFO Occupants,* by Coral and Jim Lorenzen

Reliability: 2

Narrative: The witness, identified in the literature as C.A.V. because he wished to remain anonymous, had been in Pucusana on business. While driving about six miles south of Lima, Peru, he spotted a disc-shaped object hovering 6 or 7 feet off the ground. He stopped his car and got out, thinking that he would walk over to see what it was. The distance was greater than he thought.

When he reached the object, which he described as sand-colored and very shiny, three figures emerged from it. C.A.V. saw no door or hatch, but the creatures seemed to have come from inside the craft.

Roswell, New Mexico:

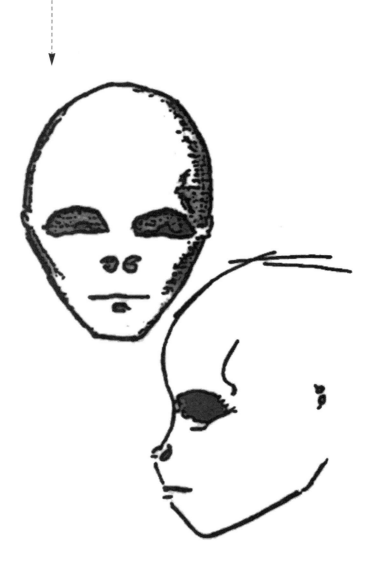

Location: Roswell, New Mexico

Witnesses: Glenn Dennis (age 22)

Encounter Type: CE-III (secondhand)

Craft Type: Unknown

Alien Type: Humanoid

Alien Characteristics: The creatures were smaller than humans, no more than 5 feet tall, with large heads and large eyes. There was no sign of ears, but there were two small holes on the sides of the head where the ears would have been. There was not much of a nose, the mouth was a slit with no lips.

The bodies were thin and the bone structure was lightweight. The arms and legs were thin. The distance between the elbow and the shoulder was shorter than the distance between the elbow and the wrist. The hands had four digits and no thumbs. The fingers were very long and slender and had small "sucker pads" on them. (The description suggests that the aliens resemble the creatures from the 1953 movie *War of the Worlds*. Of particular note are the very thin arms, the hands without thumbs, and the sucker pads on the fingertips.)

Home World: Unknown

Sources: *The UFO Crash at Roswell* and *The Truth About the UFO Crash at Roswell,* by Kevin D. Randle and Donald R. Schmitt.

Reliability: 0

Narrative: Glenn Dennis reported that a nurse he knew at the Roswell Army Air Field, Naomi Self (or Selff), was witness to a number of small, alien bodies that were brought to the base hospital. She was in a hallway when a doctor unknown to her called her into a room to assist. According to Dennis, who allegedly heard the story a day or so later, she was confronted by the bodies of three alien creatures. All were dead and seemed to have been injured in some sort of traumatic incident. Two of the bodies were mangled, but the third was more nearly intact.

None of the medical people could stay with the bodies long because a terrible odor permeated the room. They rotated in and out, but the stench soon overwhelmed them. They zipped the bodies into mortuary bags and stored them.

Dennis, at the base on another errand, walked into the hospital to look for Naomi Self. She warned him that he had better get out because he would get into serious trouble. Dennis wanted to know what had happened but was grabbed by MPs. Before he was thrown out of the hospital, he was confronted by a nasty officer with red hair. The officer warned Dennis not to say a word about anything he had seen at the base that day. He was not to go into town and shoot his mouth off.

A day or two later Dennis and Naomi Self had lunch together at the officers' club. According to Dennis, she told him that she had seen a horrible sight. She drew a sketch of the alien bodies, making it clear that she had never before seen anything like these

14

creatures. She was so sickened by the event that even a day or so later she was unable to eat. She left the officers' club, heading back to her quarters so that she could rest. Dennis never saw her again.

He did receive a note from her after she was abruptly transferred from Roswell. She was on a stopover on the East Coast and let him know her APO (Army Post Office) number so that he could write to her. His letter to her came back marked "Deceased," and he was told she had been killed, along with four other nurses, in an aircraft accident.

Dennis later lost the letter and other documentation when he left the employ of Ballard's Funeral Home. Intensive searches of military records have failed to corroborate his claim that a nurse by the name of Naomi Self ever served at the Roswell base. Searches of other sources, including the *New York Times* and *Stars and Stripes,* have failed to produce any articles or reports about an aircraft accident killing five army nurses.

Dennis now suggests that researchers have failed to find the nurse because he did not supply us with the correct name. However, other parts of Dennis's story have also collapsed under objective research.

Roswell, New Mexico:

JULY 4, 1947

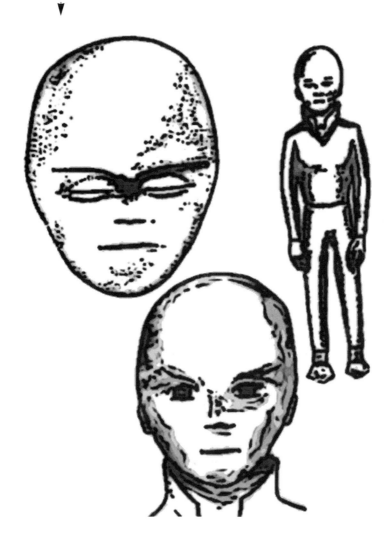

Location: Roswell, New Mexico

Witnesses: Major Edwin Easley
Dr. W. Curry Holden
Frank Kaufmann
Lieutenant Colonel Albert Lovejoy Duran
Thomas Gonzales

Encounter Type: CE-III

Craft Type: Small triangular craft.

Alien Type: Humanoid

Alien Characteristics: The bodies were described as slender and 4½ to 5 feet tall, with heads that were slightly larger than they would have been on a human of that height. The arms and legs were long and thin. The eyes of the creatures were slightly larger than human eyes and did have pupils. The facial features were similar to those of a human. There was no hair, but the skull was covered by fuzz. One of the witnesses said that the facial expressions were quite peaceful. The skin color was a gray, not unlike that of Data, the character on *Star Trek: The Next Generation*.

Home World: Unknown

Sources: *The Truth About the UFO Crash at Roswell,* by Kevin D. Randle and Donald R. Schmitt; *Conspiracy of Silence,* by Kevin D. Randle.

Reliability: 9

Narrative: Dr. W. Curry Holden, a professor of history and anthropology at Texas Tech University in Lubbock, Texas, appeared on the scene of the Roswell crash with a number of his students on the morning of July 5. Holden was searching for sites of archaeological significance in the area north of Roswell. Later Holden would say that he was there and saw the craft and the bodies, but he didn't expand much beyond that, except to confirm that the crash site was north of Roswell, not far from Highway 285 and that he saw bodies of alien creatures. He also suggested that he saw a bright, flaming light in the night sky a few hours earlier.

Major Edwin Easley, provost marshal of the 509th Bomb Group stationed at the Roswell Army Air Field in 1947, arrived at the crash site with the first group of military personnel and ordered his men to the top of the ridges overlooking the site. He ordered the entire area cordoned off and held everyone else back, away from the craft, while it was checked for radiation and other forms of contamination. The 509th Bomb Group, at that time, had the equipment necessary to deal with radiation because of its status as a nuclear strike force.

Although Easley didn't say much about the events, he did, in fact, say that the craft was of extraterrestrial origin, and he did tell family members that he had seen "the creatures." Easley's involvement has been corroborated by family members and other officers who served with him at Roswell.

18

Frank Kaufmann, another member of the 509th, was with the original group. Kaufmann saw the craft stuck into the ground at an angle. According to him, the craft was heel-shaped, with a tear in the side that allowed him to see into the interior.

Military cars and trucks were parked around the impact site as if to screen it from view. While a man in a radiation suit checked the area for contamination, the rest of the team stood back a hundred yards or more, smoking cigarettes, watching, and waiting. Once it was determined there was no radiation, photographers recorded the scene in close-up shots, and then the men moved in to begin the recovery operation.

The craft, according to a number of the eyewitnesses, was 20 to 25 feet wide. The trailing edge was slightly scalloped, and the nose was rounded. The front was damaged by the impact with the ground.

Easley, another officer, and an NCO interviewed the archaeologists, telling them that they were on the scene of an event that could threaten national security. The archaeologists were moved away from the crash site so that they were facing away from the craft and the bodies. They were questioned about all they had seen and then taken to the air base south of Roswell for further interrogation.

Thomas Gonzales, an NCO assigned to one of the transportation units at Roswell, said that he was a guard on the military cordon at the crash site. He saw the craft, which he said looked like an airfoil. He also spoke of the "little men" who had piloted the craft.

The bodies—one sitting near a cliff, another at the side of the craft, and three more inside it—were later removed, and placed in lead-lined body bags. These were then loaded into military field ambulances to be taken to the base at Roswell.

The bodies were described by the various military eyewitnesses as slender and 4½ to 5 feet tall, with heads that were slightly larger than they would have been on a human. The arms were long and thin, the distance between the wrist and elbow longer than the distance between the elbow and shoulder. The eyes of the creatures were slightly larger than human eyes, and the facial features were similar to those of a human. There was no hair, but the skull was covered with fuzz. To those assembled at the impact site it was clear that the beings were not human, nor were they the remains of humans who had been exposed to fire and abrupt changes in atmospheric pressure as a result of the crash. Edwin Easley would later tell family members only that he had seen "the creatures."

There is no reliable corroboration of the stories of an attempted preliminary autopsy at the Roswell base. The bodies were stored in a hangar, and then, under cover of darkness, were loaded on aircraft to be flown out. One aircraft was sent to Washington, D.C., so that the highest-ranking members of the government would have an opportunity to see them. The other craft was sent directly to Wright Field, in Dayton, Ohio, where the army had the facilities to study the wreckage.

One of the First:

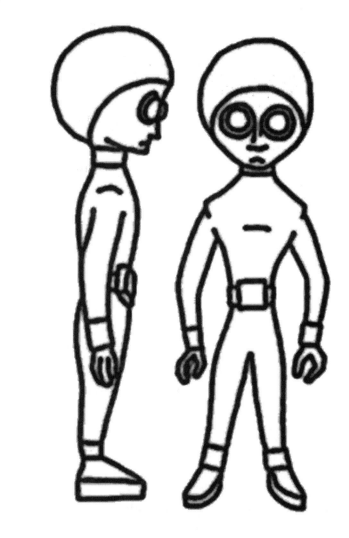

Location: Friuli, Italy

Witnesses: Professor R. L. Johannis

Encounter Type: CE-III

Craft Type: Disc

Alien Type: Humanoid

Alien Characteristics: This witness spoke of two creatures, which he described as boys. They were small, about 3 feet tall, with heads that were larger than the normal head of a human. The creatures had no hair and were wearing tight-fitting brown caps. Their noses were straight and long. The eyes were large, protuberant, and round; they were yellow-green and had a vertical pupil like that of a cat. The hands had eight fingers and seemed to be opposed.

Home World: Unknown

Sources: *The Humanoids*, by Charles Bowen.

Reliability: 6

Narrative: The witness was on a rock-hunting expedition in the mountains in the extreme northeastern part of Italy. As he was walking in the country, he emerged from a stand of trees and saw, on a rocky riverbank, a large red object that seemed to be shaped like a lens. He couldn't see it well and put on his glasses. It was clear to him that the craft was something unusual.

The witness and the creatures approached one another, but when they were a few paces apart, they stopped. The witness suddenly seemed to have no strength. Although paralyzed, he could still observe the details. Thinking about it later, he believed that he stood near the creature for only two or three minutes.

Eventually one of the creatures raised its right hand to its belt. There was a puff of smoke or a ray of some kind, and the witness fell to the ground. The rock hunter's pick that he had held was yanked from his hand as if by some invisible force.

The two creatures walked closer and picked up the pick. The witness made a "fantastic" effort and managed to sit up. As he braced himself with his hands so that he wouldn't collapse, the two creatures climbed into the craft, which then shot into the air.

ONE OF THE FIRST

Flatwoods, West Virginia:

Location: Flatwoods, West Virginia

Witnesses: Kathleen May
                Neil Numley (age 14)
                Eugene Lemon (17)
                Eddie May (13)
                Fred May (12)
                Ronnie Shaver (10)
                Tommy Hyer (10)

Encounter Type: CE-III

Craft Type: Unknown

Alien Type: Humanoid

Alien Characteristics: The creature was humanoid, with a round blood-red face. Greenish orange beams projected from two eyelike sockets. Around the face was a dark, pointed, hoodlike shape. The upper torso was clothed in a dark fabric, which some witnesses said was green.

Home World: Unknown

Sources: "The Monster and the Saucer," by Gray Barker in *Fate*, January 1953, Project Blue Book Files; *They Knew Too Much About Flying Saucers*, by Gray Barker; *Uninvited Visitors*, by Ivan T. Sanderson; *Project Blue Book*, by Brad Steiger; "You Can't Get One Out at Night by Hisself," by E. Clark in *Washington Daily News*, September 19, 1952; "The West Virginia Monster," by George Smithowski as told to Paul Lieb in *Male*, July 1955.

Reliability: 5

Narrative: It began at night when three boys saw a ball of slow-moving red light descend behind a hill near Flatwoods, West Virginia. As they headed toward what might have been the landing site, they were joined by Kathleen May; her sons, Eddie and Fred; and a seventeen-year-old member of the National Guard, Eugene Lemon.

As they walked up the hill, Lemon's dog ran ahead of them and began barking. A moment later the dog ran back down the hill, clearly frightened. At about the same time, the group ran into a foul-smelling mist that stung their eyes and noses.

They pressed on, however, and at the top of the hill Lemon and one of the boys spotted a ball of light as large as a house. To the left were two smaller lights. Lemon turned his flashlight on it, and the hideous face of a creature was suddenly visible. It began to move toward them, then turned and floated toward the ball of light.

Thirty minutes later, after all of the witnesses had walked back down the hill, a local newspaper reporter tried to interview some of them. He persuaded Lemon to accompany him back to the area, where the foul odor still lingered, but in the dark, neither Lemon nor the reporter could see anything.

The next morning the reporter returned to the site and found skid marks on the ground. They led down the hill to an area where the grass was matted in a circle about 15 feet in diameter. Investigation revealed a greaselike residue on the plants.

The Hairy Attacker:

NOVEMBER 28, 1954

Location: Caracas, Venezuela

Witnesses: Gustave Gonzales
José Ponce

Encounter Type: Attempted abduction

Craft Type: Glowing sphere

Alien Type: Hairy humanoid

Alien Characteristics: The creatures were described as about 3 feet tall and covered with stiff, bristly hair. They appeared to be extremely light, weighing as little as 35 pounds. The hands had retractable claws. The bodies were extremely hard.

Home World: Unknown

Sources: *Flying Saucers: The Startling Evidence of the Invasion from Outer Space,* by Coral E. Lorenzen; *Encounters with UFO Occupants,* by Coral and Jim Lorenzen; *The Flying Saucer Conspiracy,* by Donald Keyhoe.

Reliability: 4

Narrative: While driving to Petare, about twenty minutes away, the two witnesses spotted a glowing object about 10 feet in diameter that nearly blocked the road. Gonzales stopped, and the two men got out to investigate. A small hairy man approached, and Gonzales grabbed him, hoping to take him to the police. The creature fought back, shoving Gonzales, hurling him away.

Ponce, frightened by the encounter, ran toward the police station, only a couple of blocks away. As he ran, he saw two more little creatures, both carrying rocks and chunks of dirt, jump into the sphere.

Now the first little creature, with its claws out, attacked Gonzales. Pulling out his knife, Gonzales fought back, stabbing at the alien. The knife struck the attacker's shoulder but slipped off, as if the creature were made of solid metal.

A second creature stepped from the craft and shot a beam of light at Gonzales. Momentarily blinded, he stumbled back, away from the first alien. The two creatures then retreated and boarded the craft, which shot into the air.

Gonzales ran to the police station where both he and Ponce were suspected of being drunk. An examination revealed scratches on Gonzales. A couple of days later a doctor confirmed that he had seen the fight but hadn't remained on the scene; he didn't want to get involved.

Kelly and Hopkinsville, Kentucky:

Location: Seven miles north of Hopkinsville, Kentucky, near the small town of Kelly, sometimes called Kelly Station.

Witnesses: Glennie Lankford (age 50)
Elmer "Lucky" Sutton (25)
Vera Sutton (29)
John Charley "J.C." Sutton (21)
Alene Sutton (27)
Billy Ray Taylor (21)
June Taylor (18)
O. P. Baker (30)
Lonnie Lankford (12)
Charlton Lankford (10)
Mary Lankford (7)

Encounter Type: CE-III

Craft Type: Disc

Alien Type: Humanoid

Alien Characteristics: Small, 3½ feet tall, with big round head and large luminous eyes. The arms were slender, extending almost to the ground, with huge talonlike hands. The eyes glowed with a yellowish light. The body seemed to be made of, or covered with, silver that glowed in the dark.

Home World: Unknown

Sources: Project Blue Book Files, *Close Encounter at Kelly and Others of 1955,* by Isabel Davis and Ted Bloecher; *The UFO Encyclopedia,* by John Spencer; *The Encyclopedia of UFOs,* edited by Ronald D. Story; *Emergence of a Phenomenon: UFOs from the Beginning Through 1959,* by Jerome Clark.

Reliability: 7

Although skeptics have labeled this report as a hoax, there is no solid evidence of that. This is a multiple-witness case involving interaction with the local police authorities.

Narrative: In the early evening of August 21, 1955, Billy Ray Taylor, a young friend of Elmer "Lucky" Sutton, went to the well behind the Suttons' farmhouse and came running back to say that he had seen a flying saucer. He described the object as bright with an exhaust that contained all the colors of the rainbow. It had passed over the house, he said, then continued over the fields, and finally hovered, then descended and disappeared into a gully.

Present in the Sutton house that night were Glennie Lankford, Lucky Sutton, Vera Sutton, John Charley "J.C" Sutton, Alene Sutton, three Sutton children, June Taylor, and O. P. Baker. None of them believed the story that Lucky told them, and none of them considered walking out to the gully to see if something might be down there.

Not long after Taylor told his story, however, the dog began to bark. Taylor and Lucky Sutton went to investigate, but the dog ran under the house and did not reappear that night.

Out in the fields, away from the house, the two men saw a strange glow. As it approached, they saw a "small man" inside it. He was about 3½ feet tall, with a large head that looked to be round, and long, thin arms that extended almost to the ground. The creature's hands were large and out of proportion and were shaped more like a bird's talons than a human hand. The eyes were large and seemed to glow with a yellow fire.

As the creature continued to move toward the house, the two men retreated, found a rifle and a shotgun, and then waited. When the being came within 20 feet of the back door, both men fired. The creature flipped back, regained its feet, and fled into the darkness.

The two men watched for a few minutes and then walked into the living room where the others waited. The creature, or one just like it, appeared at one of the windows, and the men shot at it, hitting it. This one also did a backflip and disappeared.

Now the men decided to go out to learn if they had injured or killed the creature. Billy Ray Taylor was the first one out, but he stopped on the porch under a small overhang. A clawlike hand reached down and touched his hair. Alene Taylor grabbed Billy Ray to pull him back into the house. Lucky pushed past them and fired up at the creature, which was on the roof, knocking it from its perch.

Someone, probably Taylor, shouted, "There's one up in the tree."

Both Taylor and Lucky shot at it, knocking it off the limb. But it didn't fall to the ground. Instead, it seemed to float. They shot again, and it ran off into the weeds.

At the same moment another creature, possibly the one that had been on the roof, appeared around the corner of the house. Lucky whirled and fired. The buckshot sounded as if it had hit something metallic, like an empty bucket. Like the others, the creature flipped over, scrambled to its feet, and fled, moving rapidly.

Having failed to stop the creatures with either shotguns or a

.22-caliber rifle, Lucky decided to leave them alone. Someone noticed that the creatures always approached from dark areas. It seemed that they were repelled by the light.

At some point Billy Ray and Lucky heard noises on the roof and went out the back door to investigate. One of the creatures was back on the roof. They shot at it and knocked it off the roof, but it floated to a fence some 40 feet away. Hit by another shot, it fell from the fence and ran away, seeming to use its arms for locomotion.

Some of the others in the house were still unconvinced, believing that the boys were playing a prank. Glennie Lankford, who was fifty at the time, asked Taylor what he was seeing. With the lights in the house turned out, they had taken up a position close to one of the windows.

After twenty minutes or so, one of the creatures approached the front of the house. According to Lankford, it looked like a 5-gallon gasoline can with a head on top and thin, spindly legs. It shimmered as if made of bright metal.

Glennie Lankford, who had been crouching quietly for a long time, tried to stand up but fell with a thud. She shrieked and the creature jumped backward. Taylor fired at it through the screen door.

Although they thought they had driven the creatures off a number of times, the beings kept returning. The people in the house were becoming more frightened; the children were close to panic.

At about eleven o'clock that night, three hours after the first creature was seen, everyone ran to the cars. One of the kids was screaming and had to be carried. They raced to the Hopkinsville police station for help.

At the police station, there was no doubt that the people had been frightened by something. Police officers and the chief, Russell Greenwell, who were interviewed after the event, made it clear they believed the people had been scared by something.

Within minutes the police were on their way back to the house with some of the witnesses. The police also called the Madison-

34

ville headquarters of the Kentucky State Police. A call was even made to Chief Greenwell at home. He was told that a spaceship had landed at Kelly. He told the desk sergeant that it had better not be a joke.

By now Kentucky State Police, local police, the chief, and a sheriff's deputy were either heading out to the Sutton house or were already there. One of the state troopers, who was only a few miles from Hopkinsville, on the road to Kelly, said that he heard "several meteors" flash over his car. They moved with a sound like artillery, and he looked up in time to see two of them traveling in a slightly descending arc, heading toward the Sutton house.

The yard was suddenly filled with cars and, more importantly, light. The witnesses tried to point out where events had taken place. The chief searched for signs that witnesses had been drinking but found nothing to indicate that anyone had even a beer. Glennie Lankford said that she didn't allow alcohol in the house.

Once the police arrived, the situation changed. Although the atmosphere was charged and some of the police were nervous, they began to search for signs of the invasion. There were apparent bullet and buckshot holes in the window screens, and there was evidence that weapons had been fired, but there was no trace of the alien creatures. The hard-packed ground did not take footprints.

A search of the yard and fields around the house revealed little except a luminous patch where one of the creatures had fallen. It was visible from only one angle. The chief said that he saw it himself, and there was definitely some kind of stain on the grass.

But with no other evidence to be found, no alien creatures running around, and no spacecraft hidden in the gully, the police began to return to their regular duties. By two in the morning, only the Suttons were left at the house.

A newspaper photographer and his wife had accompanied the police to the Sutton house. The wife had said that she hoped to see one of the creatures but was disappointed. But a half an hour or so after the last of the police had left, when the lights were out,

Glennie Lankford saw one of the creatures looking in the window. She alerted her son, Lucky, who wanted to shoot at it, but she told him not to. She didn't want a repeat of the earlier situation. Besides, the creatures had done nothing to harm anyone during the first episode.

Lucky fired anyway. The shot was no more effective than those fired earlier. The little creatures bounced up and ran away.

They kept reappearing throughout the night, the last sighting occurring just a half an hour before sunrise.

Argentina:

1957

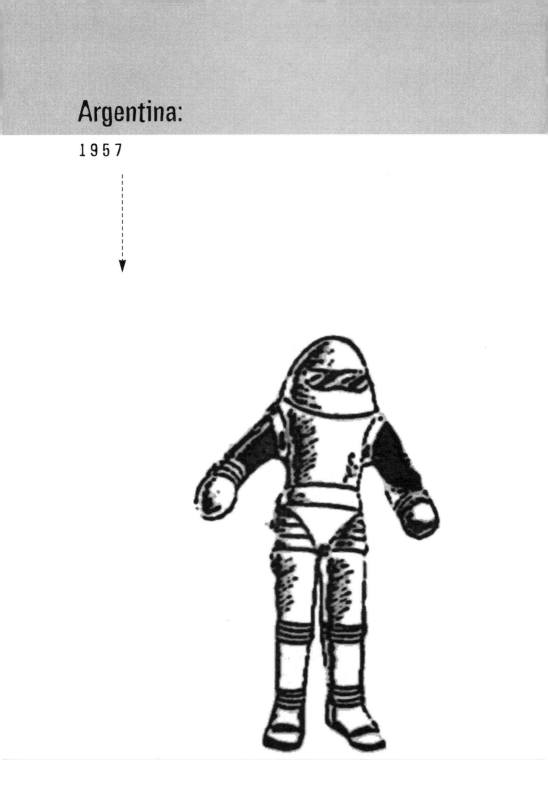

Location: Argentina

Witnesses: Not reported

Encounter Type: CE-III

Craft Type: Unknown

Alien Type: Humanoid

Alien Characteristics: The being was wearing a stiff-limbed suit that allowed only limited mobility. The arms didn't flex, though the knees did. The being inside bore a resemblance to the modern grays.

Home World: Unknown

Reliability: 0

Narrative: Like so many of the other reports that have come from Argentina, the information about this creature is sketchy. This report is rated zero because the creature is recognizable to science-fiction fans as the invading alien from the 1956 movie *Earth vs. the Flying Saucers.*

ARGENTINA

The Metaluna Monster:

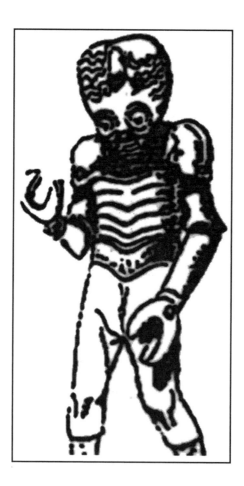

Location: Argentina

Witnesses: Not reported

Encounter Type: CE-III

Craft Type: Unknown

Alien Type: Humanoid

Alien Characteristics: This was a nonspeaking alien being with a large head, big round eyes, and hands that looked as if they were designed to serve as pincers. The creature was close to 7 feet tall.

Home World: Metaluna

Reliability: 0

Narrative: Information about this report is sketchy at best. It was among several dozen that came from South American sources, and it was reported there. The reliability is rated at zero because the creature—or, in this case, the monster—is recognizable to those of us who have watched science-fiction movies from the 1950s. There is no doubt that this creature was inspired by the "mutants" used for manual labor on Metaluna, the home world of the alien scientists in *This Island Earth* (1954).

The Holloman AFB Landing:

APRIL 25, 1964

Location: Holloman Air Force Base, New Mexico

Witnesses: Robert Emenegger
Clifford Stone

Encounter Type: CE-III

Craft Type: Classic disc

Alien Type: Human-looking

Alien Characteristics: The three "men" were dressed in tight-fitting jumpsuits. They were about 5 feet 2 and had a blue-gray complexion, wide-set catlike eyes with a vertical pupil, and large noses.

Home World: Unknown

Sources: *Alien Contact,* by Timothy Good; *The Emergence of a Phenomenon: UFOs from the Beginning Through 1959,* by Jerome Clark; and *UFOs Past, Present and Future,* by Robert Emenegger.

Reliability: 3

Narrative: Although there is a controversy as to the date of the event, most researchers suggest that on April 25, 1964, at 5:30 in the morning, about twelve hours after the Lonnie Zamora sighting near Socorro, New Mexico, a landing took place at Holloman Air Force Base.

Alien craft were spotted by Holloman radar and were warned off but apparently landed anyway. The base commander ordered an alert. Two interceptors were sent up to chase the alien ships from the area. The base commander supposedly alerted officers at both Wright-Patterson and Edwards Air Force Bases.

There were three disc-shaped craft. One of them landed on the airfield at Holloman while the other two stayed aloft. A sliding door of some kind opened, and a ramp extended. Three alien beings, dressed in jumpsuits and wearing some type of headdress, exited. Apparently a group of military officers were there to meet with the alien creatures. Communication with the creatures was possible because of some kind of small device they carried.

An air force crew was there to film the sequence, and a number of people have claimed to have seen this film. Supposedly this film was intended to be used as part of a documentary to announce the presence of aliens on Earth. Clifford Stone, a UFO researcher living in Roswell, New Mexico, claimed that as an army enlisted man, he saw the film under strict security.

It should be noted that some have reported the date of the landing as 1971, though most researchers accept the 1964 date. According to some researchers, the purpose of the contact was to reclaim the bodies of beings killed when their craft crashed outside of Roswell in 1947.

It was at this landing that some kind of agreement between the U.S. government and the aliens was allegedly reached. Rumors about the content of that agreement have been circulating throughout the UFO community for years. No documentation is available, however, nor has good corroborative evidence for that claim been found.

Big Nose in a Dunce Hat:

Location: Imjarvi, Mikkeli, Finland

Witnesses: Aaron Heinonen (age 36)
      Esko Viljo (38)

Encounter Type: CE-III

Craft Type: Spherical

Alien Type: Humanoid

Alien Characteristics: The creature was slender and about 3 feet tall, with narrow sloping shoulders and thin arms and legs. The face was a waxy white, with small eyes, a large hooked nose, and small pointed ears. It wore light green coveralls, dark green boots, and white gloves. It also wore a pointed duncelike cap and carried a small box with a lens or opening in the front.

Home World: Unknown

Sources: *APRO Bulletin;* "A Humanoid Was Seen at Imjarvi," by Sven-Olaf Fredickson in *Flying Saucer Review.*

Reliability: 3

Narrative: The witnesses, who had been skiing, heard a buzzing sound and saw a bright light in the sky. The light was then engulfed by a reddish gray mist with smoke puffing from the top.

As the cloud neared the ground, both Viljo and Heinonen noticed a metallic sphere inside it. Under the sphere were three hemispheres and a central tube. When the buzzing ceased, the cloud disappeared and the object hovered about 10 feet above the ground. A light from the tube shone on the ground, creating a circle about 3 feet in diameter. Inside the beam of light, standing on the ground, was a 3-foot-tall creature holding a small box at waist height.

The creature eventually pointed the box at Heinonen. As he did so, a thick, reddish gray mist came from the object. Huge, long red, green, and purple sparks shot from the circle of light on the snow. Although the sparks hit both the men, they felt nothing. The mist continued to thicken, finally obscuring the small creature.

After several minutes the light beam seemed to retract into the tube, the mist disappeared, and the air around them cleared. Heinonen felt his side go numb, and when he tried to take a step, he fell. Viljo helped him return to the cottage. There he became increasingly ill with vomiting, loss of memory, and fever. The symptoms continued for months.

Viljo also became ill, but his symptoms were not as severe as those manifested by his friend. His face reddened and was swollen, he had trouble maintaining his balance, and he reported pain in his eyes. A doctor who examined both men reported that the symptoms resembled those of radiation poisoning.

Although an interested reporter was able to locate two others who claimed to have seen the craft, there was no corroboration for the sighting of the strange humanoid. To make the report even less credible, Heinonen claimed to have seen alien craft on a number of other occasions and to have made contact with alien pilots.

The Malaysia Creature:

Location: Bukit Mertajam, Penang, Malaysia

Witnesses: Mohamed Ali
             Abdul Rahim
             David Tan
             K. Wigneswaran
             Mohamad Zulkifli

Encounter Type: CE-III

Craft Type: Unknown

Alien Type: Humanoid

Alien Characteristics: Extremely small creatures, about 3 inches tall. The one identified as the leader had horns on his head and was dressed in yellow.

Home World: Unknown

Sources: "A Wave of Small Humanoids in Malaysia," in *Flying*

Saucer Review, June 1983; *The UFO Phenomenon: Mysteries of the Unknown,* Time-Life Books.

Reliability: 2

Narrative: Several boys were playing in the vicinity of Stowell English Primary School when a "soup-plate-sized" flying saucer landed near them. A plank was put out, and five tiny spacemen emerged. Four of them wore blue uniforms, but the fifth was dressed in yellow with stars on its shirt.

Ignoring the boys, the spacemen began to rig an antenna on a nearby tree. One of the boys, Wigneswaran, decided to capture the leader, but the tiny creature fired a miniature "ray gun" at him. The other boys fled in terror, abandoning their friend, who was later found in the bushes by one of the school officials. There was a small red dot on his right leg where he had been struck by a ray from the weapon.

Although the headmaster believed the story to be a figment of the boys' imaginations, they insisted it was true.

Las Cruces, New Mexico:

Location: 23 miles east of Deming, New Mexico

Witnesses: Hilda McAfee (age, late 50s)

Encounter Type: CE-III

Craft Type: Unknown

Alien Type: Humanoid

Alien Characteristics: Two male humanoids of about average height but rather stocky were dressed in bulky pale blue quilted coveralls. They were wearing wide belts and gloves that matched the coveralls. Each wore boots that reached about halfway up the calf. They wore helmets with dark visors so that no facial features could be seen. Both of the creatures appeared to be rigid.

Home World: Unknown

Sources: *APRO Bulletin,* December 1975.

Reliability: 8   There is a very real possibility that what these two women saw was some type of American experimental craft. The size of the aliens reported, the location where they were reported, and the clothing they wore all suggest an American experiment. The fact the aliens turned on their lights at the approach of the car also supports this belief.

Narrative: Hilda McAfee and her elderly mother were on their way home from Las Cruces, New Mexico. About 23 miles east of Deming, a bright blue light flashed on them from a short distance away. It seemed to be coming from their lane on Interstate 10. The light was bright and blinding.

McAfee saw an object ahead of her and prepared to pull around it. She and her mother saw two creatures standing under a craft that neither woman could later describe. The bright light seemed to be above them, hiding the shape of the object. There were black rods about 4 or 5 inches wide near the two creatures.

The two creatures, which McAfee referred to as men, were 5½ to 6 feet tall and robust. They were dressed in identical blue coveralls, with gloves, belts, and boots to match. They both wore helmets so that no facial features could be seen. Neither seemed interested in the women, and both continued working as the car drove by them. They stood flatfooted on the pavement, and one had his back turned. He seemed to be working on something.

After they had passed, the two women looked back, but the object seemed to have disappeared. Both women believed that the lights on it had been turned on to prevent a collision. Once they were beyond the site, the lights were turned off.

Both women suffered burning, aching chest and arm pains after the encounter. Both said that even their bones seemed to hurt.

One other point might have some relevance. McAfee is the landlady of Chaney Rogers, a brother to Mike Rogers, who was involved in the Travis Walton abduction (see "The Walton Experience," page 176). It was because of that connection that McAfee decided to tell her tale. She believed that no one would laugh at her now that Walton case had received national publicity.

Another Attempted Abduction:

N OVEMBER 2, 1973

Location: Goffstown, New Hampshire

Witnesses: Lyndia Morel

Encounter Type: CE-III

Craft Type: An orange-and-gold spherical craft with an oval window and covered with a honeycomblike outer skin.

Alien Type: Catlike humanoid

Alien Characteristics: Only the upper body of the creature was visible through the window of the craft. It was described as being covered with wrinkled gray skin and having large slanted eyes.

Home World: Unknown

Sources: *APRO Bulletin*, January–February 1974; *The October Scenario*, by Kevin Randle

Reliability: 4

Narrative: On the night of November 2, 1973, Lyndia Morel saw a strange yellow light in the distance as she drove to work. She kept watching it, saying that it originally looked like a bright star. She thought that it might be a planet. As she continued to drive, the object seemed to approach slowly until she could tell that it was spherical and covered with a honeycomb except for a single oval window. Inside the window she could see the upper body of a creature with wrinkled gray skin and large slanted eyes. She believed that the body was darker than the face.

As she tried to continue driving to work, she felt her eyes drawn to the UFO. She later said that her hands seemed to be stuck to the steering wheel. She had the feeling that the object, or the being in it, was beginning to take control of her body. She became extremely frightened and wanted to get away from it.

Although she claimed that she never stopped the car, she did tell investigators that there was a short point where she experienced "a loss of memory." Morel thought that "they" might have "retrieved or recorded her memory during this interval." Suddenly she realized that her car was moving at a high speed. Of course, it is possible that she was unconsciously accelerating because of the proximity of the UFO. Believing that the object was pulling her car toward it, she became convinced that she was about to be captured.

When she noticed a house ahead of her, she pulled into a farm driveway, leaped from her car, and ran to the door. She hammered on it, screaming for help, and finally managed to awaken the house's occupants.

Once inside, she convinced the man that she wasn't crazy, but when he went out to check, the UFO was gone. Morel told the man that she believed the occupant of the craft wanted to capture her. She also persuaded him to call the local police.

Officer Daniel Jubinville responded to the call. When he arrived, he turned off the lights and engine of Morel's car, which suggested she had abandoned it quickly. He also noted in his report that it was evident Morel had been badly frightened by something.

Morel, Jubinville, and the farm couple, Mr. and Mrs. Beaudoin, went outside. They did see an object in the distance that was little more than a point of light. When Jubinville directed his flashlight at it, the object seemed to move slightly and change colors. Walter Webb, who investigated the case, didn't believe that the object seen by the four witnesses was the UFO. He noted in his report that the object seemed to be close to the position where Mars would have been in the night sky. Webb didn't think that the multiple-witness aspect of the sighting was particularly persuasive.

Vilvoorde, Belgium:

DECEMBER 19, 1973

Location: Vilvoorde, north of Brussels, Belgium

Witnesses: Mr. V

Encounter Type: CE-III

Craft Type: Small and round

Alien Type: Humanoid, robotic

Alien Characteristics: This was a small creature, about 3 feet tall, wearing a shiny one-piece suit that glowed green. Over the alien's head was a large, transparent globular helmet with a tube that ran down to a backpack. Through the helmet the witness saw two very large oval-shaped yellow eyes. The being had pointed ears, but no nose or mouth was visible. On the stomach was a large red box that seemed to be sparking. The creature was holding something that looked like a metal detector, which it was passing over the ground.

Home World: Unknown

Sources: *High Strangeness: UFOs from 1960 Through 1979,* by Jerome Clark; *World Atlas of UFOs,* by John Spencer.

Reliability: 3

Narrative: The witness, whose name has been withheld at his request, got out of bed to use the toilet, which was outside the house next to the kitchen. As he walked into the kitchen he heard a strange noise. Through the kitchen curtains he saw a greenish light, and when he pulled them aside he saw a small man using what might have been a metal detector in the garden.

The witness directed a flashlight beam on the being, which turned toward him with its entire body, rather than just its head. As the witness flashed the light, the creature raised its hand and made a *V* sign, then turned and walked off toward the tall grass near the back wall of the garden.

When it reached the rear wall, it continued walking straight up the wall, but it remained perpendicular to the surface of the wall. When it reached the top, it apparently walked down the other side of the wall. Moments later the witness saw a small craft in the distance.

VILVOORDE, BELGIUM

The Warneton Incident:

Location: Near the Franco-Belgian Border

Witnesses: Mr. X

Encounter Type: CE-III with electromagnetic effects

Craft Type: Disc with slight dome and a three-leg landing gear

Alien Type: Humanoid

Alien Characteristics: There were two figures. The taller one was about 5 feet tall and wore a boxlike helmet. The head was shaped like an inverted pear. The skin was grayish, and there were two circular eyes that looked like marbles and were slightly sunken in the eye sockets. There were eyebrows, a small nose, and a slitlike mouth with no lips.

The smaller creature was dressed in a suit that seemed to have rings around the torso. It wore a round helmet with a large area of glass on the front. It was holding a stick with a pyramid tip.

Home World: Unknown

Sources: *Encounters with UFO Occupants,* by Coral and Jim Lorenzen; *Flying Saucer Review* article by Gordon Creighton.

Reliability: 3

Narrative: The witness, identified only as Mr. X, was driving along the highway when his car engine began to stutter and his headlights failed. A moment later the engine quit, and the car coasted to a stop. As he started to get out, he noticed something standing in a field about 500 feet away. At first he thought it was nothing more than a load of hay, but then he saw areas of orangish white light on the object, which seemed to be standing on three legs. As he stared, he saw that the object looked like a British army helmet from the First World War—that is, a shallow domed disc.

Then, about 100 feet away, he saw two figures, one taller than the other. The taller being was about 5 feet tall and wore a boxlike helmet. The head was shaped like an inverted pear. The skin was grayish, and there were two circular eyes that looked like marbles and were slightly sunken in the eye sockets. There were eyebrows, a small nose, and a slitlike mouth with no lips.

The two creatures continued to move toward the witness so that he was able to see them clearly. They stopped near a ditch at the side of the road. He then felt a faint shock at the back of the head and sensed rather than heard a low-pitched modulated sound, which grew louder.

During this time, the witness thought he saw a small oval object fall from the belt of the lead creature. The witness didn't try to recover it then, but later, when he returned, the field had been plowed and the object was lost.

Both creatures then turned their heads in perfect synchronization, and seemed to look behind the witness's car. The low-pitched hum ceased, and both creatures, again in perfect synchronization, turned and headed back toward the object. The witness described their motion as almost humanlike, but he said they seemed to have no trouble moving over the muddy, wet field.

Once the creatures were inside the craft, the legs disappeared and it hovered just inches off the ground for a short period. Then it climbed out at an angle of 60 or 70 degrees and disappeared in moments.

Another car approached and stopped behind the witness's vehicle. When the driver got out, the witness asked if he, too, had seen the UFO. The driver said he had, but the witness failed to get his name for corroboration.

Bosak Encounter:

Location: Frederic, Wisconsin

Witnesses: William Bosak (age 68)

Encounter Type: CE-III

Craft Type: Unknown

Alien Type: Human

Alien Characteristics: The alien was described as human-looking, except that its ears looked more like those of a calf and it had hair sticking out from the sides of its head. It wore a skintight light brown collarless garment that resembled a diver's suit.

Home World: Unknown

Sources: *APRO Bulletin*, January–February 1975.

Reliability: 5

Narrative: William Bosak was returning to his farm late one night, driving slowly because of the patchy fog. He spotted something on the left side of the road and slowed as his headlights reflected from it. The object was 8 to 10 feet tall and contained a "transparent" glass area through which Bosak could see the creature. The object itself had no lights of its own, but reflected the headlights of his car.

Bosak nearly stopped, but then got scared. He accelerated and drove around the object. As he did so, there was a swishing sound, like tree branches brushing against the side of his car.

Bosak didn't tell anyone about the sighting for nearly a month. He finally told his wife and son. He was later interviewed by the local newspaper and APRO Field Investigator Everett E. Lightner, who said that he found Bosak to be a sincere man with a good reputation.

The Johnny Sands Case:

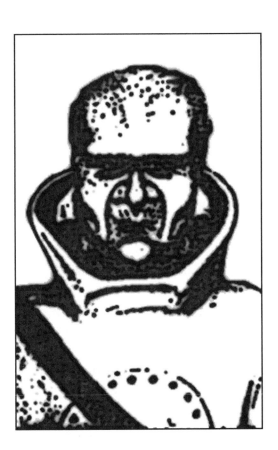

Location: Northwest of Las Vegas, Nevada

Witnesses: Johnny Sands (age 30)

Encounter Type: CE-III

Craft Type: Unknown

Alien Type: Humanoid

Alien Characteristics: The creatures were about 5 feet 7 or 5 feet 8 and weighed about 140 pounds. They were bald with no eyelashes or eyebrows and with gill-like protrusions on either side of their faces. The eyes were small and black with white pupils. The mouths were small and wrinkled and never opened. They had pug noses and "humanlike" hands with four fingers and a thumb.

Home World: Unknown

Sources: *APRO Bulletin*, March 1976.

Reliability: 1

Narrative: Johnny Sands, a country-and-western singer, was returning to Las Vegas from Pahrump on Blue Diamond Road when he saw an unusual aircraft. Although it seemed to follow him for about 3 miles, he didn't pay much attention to it. But then his car engine started sputtering, and he pulled over to the side of the road.

He got out of his car and then, looking up, saw the craft about 1,000 feet above him. He thought it was about 60 feet long and shaped like the Goodyear blimp. There were portholes, each one about 10 feet in diameter, around the circumference of the craft. The object was a rusty orange with flashing red and white lights.

As he turned back to work on his car, he looked down the road and saw two shiny figures approaching. After standing there for ten minutes watching him, they walked away into the desert. After they had gone about 200 feet, there was a flash of light and they were gone.

Sands, under questioning by researchers, did say that the creatures had asked him a number of questions. They had asked why Sands was where he was, why there were so many people in Las Vegas, and what means of communication he used. Sands said there were other topics of conversation, but he didn't want to reveal them because he felt it would be breaking a trust. The creatures had told him not to say anything about the encounter.

The Fairy Creature:

Location: Rowley Regis, West Midlands, England

Witnesses: Jean Hingley

Encounter Type: CE-III

Craft Type: Orange sphere

Alien Type: Winged humanoid

Alien Characteristics: The three beings sighted were about 3½ feet tall and sported large wings that looked paper-thin and were covered with glittering raised dots. The eyes were bright black and were set far apart on white faces. There was only a slight trace of a nose or mouth. The beings didn't seem to have hands or feet, but pointed shapes at the ends of their arms and legs. They could fly and pressed the buttons on their silver tunics at various times. When they flew, their arms were clasped over their chests and their legs hung down stiffly.

Home World: Unknown

Sources: "The Mince-Pie Martians: The Rowley Regis Case," by Alfred Budden; *The UFO Phenomenon: Mysteries of the Unknown*, Time-Life Books.

Reliability: 4

Narrative: Just after Jean Hingley watched her husband leave for work, she spotted an orange sphere close to the roof of the garage. Her dog reacted by becoming stiff and falling over. At that moment, three small beings, each about 3½ feet tall, zipped into the house making a zee-zee-zee sound. Hingley ran into the living room when she heard the Christmas tree rattling, only to find two of the creatures shaking it. Later they jumped up and down on the couch like children left alone.

During the hour-long encounter, Hingley reported that she felt periodically paralyzed. When the aliens spoke, in unison and in gruff voices, they pushed the buttons on their tunics. When she gave them orders—telling them, for instance, to stop swooping around the room—the lights on their helmets would flash, focusing a thin beam on her forehead. This burned her and occasionally blinded her. The effects of the laserlike beams persisted long after the encounter had ended.

At no point did the creatures eat or drink during the encounter, though they tried. They were unable to eat the mince pies she offered, nor could they drink the water. And they would not answer her questions about where they came from or what they were doing.

Finally the creatures flew out the door and into their orange sphere, which took off toward the north. As the creatures left, Hingley fell to the floor in pain. When she recovered, she called her husband, her neighbors, and the local police. Although no one else saw anything, an examination of the garden revealed two parallel lines, each about an inch wide, that looked like thin caterpillar tracks. Hingley reported that her television, radio, and clock had stopped working properly, and the cassette tapes that the creatures had handled were ruined. For about a week after the events, Hingley's eyes were sore. A red spot remained on her forehead for months.

Earth vs. the Flying Saucers—Again:

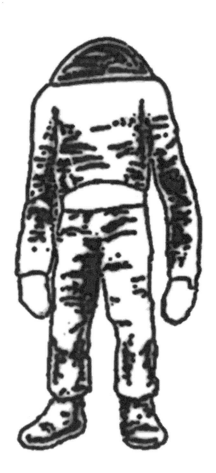

Location: Voronezh, Russia

Witnesses: Genya Blinov
               Vasya Surin
               Julia Sholokhova

Encounter Type: CE-III

Craft Type: Spherical

Alien Type: Humanoid

Alien Characteristics: The first creature sighted was about 10 feet tall, had no noticeable neck and no facial features other than three eyes. The center eye, raised above the other two, glowed red and might have been a lamp of some sort. The creature wore silver-colored coveralls and bronze-colored boots.

A second, smaller creature, or robot, accompanied the giant. It was described as square with a head on top.

Home World: Unknown

Sources: *UFO Chronicles of the Soviet Union,* by Jacques Vallee.

Reliability: 1

Narrative: On the evening of September 27, 1989, as many as fifty witnesses watched a large spherical object hover over a park. A hatch opened in the bottom revealing a humanoid creature about 10 feet tall. The being seemed to have three eyes, but the middle eye was red and had no pupil.

After the creature surveyed the surrounding terrain, the hatch closed and the craft landed and settled, brushing against a tree, and the tall creature, accompanied by a smaller, robotlike being, stepped out. The creature said something, and a small glowing triangle appeared. When the giant spoke again, the triangle disappeared.

One of the witnesses, a small boy, started crying, drawing the attention of the creature. The boy stopped crying, afraid to move. When others in the crowd began to shout, the craft and creatures vanished, but they reappeared about five minutes later. Now the 10-foot creature held a tube, which it pointed at a teenage boy, who immediately disappeared. The creature then entered the craft, and it lifted off. As it vanished, the boy reappeared.

Some of those present reported a symbol on the belt buckle of the tall alien, known as UMMO. Most believe the UMMO sightings, which originated in Spain in the 1970s, are part of an elaborate hoax.

Part II

The Contactees

Long before the first reported abduction, people were claiming to have conversed with creatures from outer space. To try to understand the contactees we must take a look at the period in history when this phenomenon occurred—the years from 1947 to the present. The attitudes, the fears, and the paranoia of this era all combined to create a perfect atmosphere for reports of contact with benevolent space brothers who claimed they were concerned with our well-being.

The contactee movement was born soon after the flying saucer rage of 1947. The common thread among all of the contactees was the spiritual aspect of the message and the method of contact. Most often the contact was made telepathically through a channeler or a medium. The message was then passed down to the contactee's followers at regularly scheduled meetings or at flying saucer conferences. The message was most often something on the order of "Be good to each other. Be kind to the planet. You are not alone." That simple message was perfect for a Cold War era marked by fear and uncertainty about the future.

Three basic fears combined to form the perfect environment for alien intervention through messages to contactees. First, there was the fear of apocalypse. Since the dawn of recorded history, men have preached the end of the world. As early as 650 B.C. Zarathustra suggested that the world would end in an ordeal by fire. The prophet Ezekiel in 587 B.C. predicted that Egypt would be so totally destroyed that nothing would be able to live there for forty years. The Bible abounds with vivid predictions of the violent end of the world.

The decade of the fifties was a time of anxiety, paranoia, naïveté, and plenty. As a nation we were prospering. The American Dream was alive and well. But for the first time in our history we had developed a weapon that brought the idea of apocalypse out of the Bible and into the newspaper.

The public had little understanding of atomic energy, and many felt that toying with it would lead to global destruction. This fear was so widespread that bomb shelters were being built all over the country. The fear was so deeply embedded in the public that some housing tracts in the Southwest used bomb shelters as a selling point. Drop-and-cover was taught in our schools, and on the first Friday of each month Civil Defense sirens rang out test warnings in every town and city across the U.S.A.

Of course, the fear of apocalypse was only made more real by the second great fear—the Communists. It was the beginning of the Cold War, and many people were convinced that the scourge of communism would soon destroy us. Senator Joseph McCarthy was spreading paranoia throughout the land. He had the nation convinced that the Communists were secretly taking over. Paranoia and fear of invasion by Communists became part of the very fabric of society.

And that takes us to another fear—flying saucers. It's easy to see, as we look back on that era, just how important flying saucers were: the largest magazines in the country—*Life, Look, Time,* and the *Saturday Evening Post*—all ran UFO stories, newspapers were full of reports of sightings, and the most popular comedians of the day told flying saucer jokes.

Many people believed that the saucers were here as the result of our development and use of the atomic bomb. The arrival of the atomic age had led many people to speculate that the aliens were here to intervene in our use of atomic energy.

This fear of atomic energy was so widespread that it actually led David Lilienthal, the chairman of the Atomic Energy Commission, to state publicly that the UFOs had nothing to do with atomic testing.

In 1949, Sidney Shallett wrote a two-part article on UFOs, which appeared in the *Saturday Evening Post.* In it he said that Americans were living in a "jittery age" induced by "atomic psychosis."

As a nation we felt helpless against the awesome power of the hydrogen bomb, and we feared the invisible but ever-present Communist threat. At the same time, man was on the threshold of space. It now seemed clear that we would soon be sending rockets to other planets. All of these circumstances contributed to the belief that the galactic federation would soon intervene to save us from ourselves.

The motion picture industry was quick to cash in on people's fears, and the movies of that period now provide a fictional record of the fears of the time. Many of the science-fiction films of this era depict attacks by creatures that were mutated by the atom. Movies like *It Came From Beneath the Sea, Rodan, Attack of the 50 Ft. Woman, The Amazing Colossal Man,* and *Attack of the Crab Monsters* were all warnings of the destruction that atomic testing would bring.

The films about flying saucers and aliens also centered around these fears or on the belief that the aliens were trying to save us from ourselves. In *Rocket Ship X-M*, the Martians told us how their planet was destroyed by atomic war. In *The Day the Earth Stood Still,* an allegory about the return of Christ, the planetary federation comes to Earth to save us from destroying ourselves with atomic energy.

While these films echoed our fear of atomic energy, films like *Invasion of the Body Snatchers, Killers from Space,* and *Invaders from Mars* addressed our fear of secret invasion by the scourge of communism. In these films the aliens find us unsuspecting and unable to protect ourselves as the silent invasion takes over our country.

At the same time many books about flying saucers began to appear. These books presented what the authors claimed was hard factual evidence that the saucers were here. The flying saucer books of this period all reflected the theme of the atomic threat and interplanetary intervention.

In *The Riddle of the Flying Saucers,* published in 1950, the author suggested that the atom bomb would destroy the world or even make the sun explode. Donald Keyhoe, in *Flying Saucers Are Real,* suggested that several bombs set off at the same time could actually knock the Earth out of its orbit. In *Flying Saucers from Outer Space,* Keyhoe stated that the Russians would launch a massive atom bomb attack on the United States in 1954. Then, in 1955, Harold Wilkins wrote in *Flying Saucers Uncensored* that the saucers had come to Earth because the atom bomb was destroying the planet's crust.

This mix of paranoia, fear, and helplessness mixed with religion fueled the contactee phenomenon. George Van Tassel, George Adamski, and other contactees were offering solutions to problems that seemed insurmountable. Only extraterrestrials had the superhuman power to overcome the negative forces that mankind had brought to planet Earth.

George Van Tassel, born in Jefferson, Ohio, in 1910, had always been interested in aviation. He entered the field in 1927, when as a profession it was still in its infancy. After three years with an early midwestern airline, George went to California and was employed by Douglas Aircraft Company. He left Douglas in 1941 and became the personal flight inspector for Howard Hughes in flight tests of experimental aircraft. In 1943, George was offered a flight-inspection position at Lockheed, where he worked on the new constellation aircraft.

When George first came to California he settled in Santa Monica where his uncle Glen Pane ran a successful automotive repair business. It was at Uncle Glen's Garage that George met Frank Critzer.

Critzer has been described as a strange little man, slight of build and not physically well. He was of German extraction, and his background is unclear. Some say he was in the German U-Boat Corps in World War I; others place him in the U.S. Army. Whatever Frank's background, he was a bright man, perhaps a genius, who had some grandiose plans.

It was 1930 when Critzer pulled into Glen Pane's repair shop in his old Essex. Frank told Glen that he had to move to a drier climate on his doctor's orders because of a lung condition. He told Glen and his nephew George of his plans to move to an area in the desert called Giant Rock, where he would prospect for precious gems and minerals. If Glen would fix his Essex, Frank would share his profits with him.

Critzer must have been very convincing; Glen not only fixed the Essex but filled it with canned goods as well. He even gave Critzer thirty dollars as a grubstake.

While Glen was working on the Essex, Frank Critzer was telling young George about all of his plans. A strong bond developed between the two of them, a bond that would last until the end of Critzer's life.

A year after Glen sent Frank on his way, Glen received a postcard from Critzer inviting both Glen and George to come to Giant Rock to see what he had done. They did visit, and what they saw both amazed and thrilled them.

After a full day's trek from Santa Monica to the desolate area of the California desert called Giant Rock, they were greeted by the largest boulder that either of them had ever seen. Under that six-story-high boulder, Critzer had dug a 900-square-foot home. Using the old Essex as a tractor, he had built over 56 miles of road in the desert. Critzer had also turned a dry lake into a runway and named it the Giant Rock Airport.

Critzer told Glen and George that while he was working on his home, he had seen many planes flying overhead on their way to Palm Springs. Frank thought this would be the perfect place for the fliers to stop for a rest or repairs. Frank was right. Just like the movie *Field of Dreams*, Frank built it and they came. For ten years Frank Critzer mined for minerals and serviced the planes that landed at the Giant Rock Airport. George visited Frank as often as he could, and a close friendship grew.

Frank was not well liked by the few residents of the area, however. They called him Hermit or Beetle, because he lived under a rock. He also had a German accent, so some people assumed he must be a spy, and that's the tale that was told to the FBI and other law enforcement agencies.

It was now 1942, the United States was at war, and Frank was suspected of being a spy. It is unclear how the end came, but on a June night in 1942 two deputies from Riverside County visited Frank, who lived outside of their jurisdiction. They wanted to take him in for questioning, but Frank resisted. And this is where the story gets vague. Frank went down into his home, bolted the door behind him, and refused to go with the deputies. One story claims that Frank shouted out, "You'll never take me alive," and then committed suicide by igniting 200 pounds of TNT. According to the other story, the deputies lobbed a tear gas canister through the window in the door; the canister ignited the TNT, and so ended the life of the Hermit of Giant Rock.

George returned to Giant Rock in 1944. What he found disturbed him deeply. The home of his friend Frank Critzer had been stripped and looted. Nothing of value remained. Giant Rock Airport had been closed and was in ruin.

It's hard to say what motivated George to do what he did, but in 1945 he petitioned the Bureau of Land Management for a ninety-nine-year lease on the land comprising the Giant Rock area and the airport. George also bought a 20-acre parcel with a home about 2 miles from the rock. He then went back to Lockheed and waited for the wheels of the bureaucracy to turn.

It was a slow process even then, but finally in 1947, two years after the request, the BLM granted George Van Tassel a ninety-nine-year lease on the Giant Rock property. As soon as the lease was granted, George resigned from Lockheed and moved his wife and three children to Giant Rock and a new beginning.

Even today, nearly fifty years later, the area around Giant Rock could best be described as rural. In the 1940s you would probably have said it was isolated. What was the lure of the big boulder in the desert? What would compel a man thirty-seven years of age to give up a career in the booming aviation business and follow a dream? Was it the same power that had led Frank Critzer to settle in the middle of nowhere?

George Van Tassel had a plan. He was a man driven by a dream. The first thing he did was to clear out the home under the rock and make it more comfortable. His next move was to improve the runway and build a café next to the rock. By late 1947 the Giant Rock Airport was once again open for business. George began to announce his grandiose plans to the world.

Giant Rock Airport had the "longest private runway in the state of California" and the "largest natural grandstand" in the world. George envisioned international air shows at Giant Rock. He planned to build a nine-hole golf course, a target range, horseshoe courts, campsites, and then cabins and a swimming pool. He also said that he and a partner had many "valuable" claims on property that contained deposits of radium and other precious metals. His vision, it seemed, was to create a tourist attraction at Giant Rock, an oasis "in the middle of nowhere." As strange as that may seem, another man, a man named Walt Disney, actually did build an oasis in the middle of the California orange groves some seven years later. But George Van Tassel's dream of tourism in the desert never came to pass, at least not according to his original plan.

The golf course, cabins, and pool were never built. There is no record of any international air shows at Giant Rock, and no record has ever been found of the "valuable" mining claims. The Giant

Rock Airport and the café did provide a meager living for George and his family from 1947 to 1953, but it was nothing compared to an event that took place in 1953—an event that would change George Van Tassel and Giant Rock forever.

Yucca Valley was the city closest to Giant Rock. It was the supply hub for the area and the spiritual and religious center for the high desert. In the 1920s and 1930s an interest in the metaphysical, or the New Age, came to Yucca Valley: "Mentalphysics," a large research center designed by Frank Lloyd Wright, was built there. George took an interest and started to attend the Mentalphysics meetings. The area was steeped in Native American culture, and the New Age metaphysics embraced the Indian ways. At the meetings, George would chant and meditate. He called upon his Indian spirit guide, and in a voice that was foreign to him, a guide was channeled.

George became deeply involved in the contact with what he thought to be his spirit guide, so it came as a surprise when one day at the Giant Rock he was contacted telepathically by an entity that claimed to be from Mars. George was given many messages by his alien brothers and was told to pass them on to others.

George Van Tassel, for whatever reason, was being touched by an alien power. It came to him in the form of contact that we have come to call channeling. A being, or entity, was speaking through George, and people began to listen.

These contacts were occurring on a regular basis. The psychic messages were from a variety of starship commanders with names that were, to say the least, unique: Lutbunn, Elcar, Clota, Totalmon, Latamarx, Noma, Leektow, Luu, Singba, Clatu, and many more. The most significant of them all was Astar, not because his message was any different from the others but because Astar has been channeled by many contactees over the years.

According to George, the reason for the contact by the space brothers was to "raise humanity's vibratory attunement." To put it in simple terms, the message was "Be good to the planet, be good to each other, and don't mess with atomic bombs," but of course the actual messages were much longer. In fact, George had to write seven books and publish a monthly newsletter to get all of them out to a waiting public.

People were now traveling to Giant Rock not for the oasis in the desert but to meet the man who could see and talk to flying saucers and the people in them. The message given to George Van Tassel was so profound and timely that people flocked to Giant Rock from all the corners of the world.

George was instructed by his space brothers to form an organization to disseminate their information, and that was the basis of the formation of the Church of Universal Wisdom and the College of Universal Wisdom. These two organizations flourished throughout the 1950s and 1960s, Giant Rock became the site of an annual flying saucer convention that attracted as many as 18,000 people at a time—quite an accomplishment if you consider that the largest UFO convention today draws no more than 5,000 people at best.

The Giant Rock Spacecraft Conventions started in 1953 and were an annual event until 1968. It wasn't the vision of golf and cabins that George had once had for the Giant Rock Airport, but it was an attraction in the desert. Giant Rock Airport had become Spaceport One, or UFO Central. As a matter of fact, there was so much interest in the UFO phenomenon that in the 1957 Spacecraft Convention issue of *Thy Kingdom Come,* a publication of the Los Angeles Interplanetary Study Groups, Gabriel Green, chairman and director of the Amalgamated Flying Saucer Clubs of America, published a list of clubs and organizations that spanned the United States from coast to coast. The list included sixty-six groups in the United States and twenty-five others worldwide.

Gabriel Green's goal was to unite all of those groups into one amalgamated body that would pool information. His aim is summed up in this excerpt from that 1957 publication: "Let us amalgamate. Let us cooperate. Let us unite in our common fight against ignorance, fear, suppression of truth, mass injustices, and the workings of the organized forces of darkness. There is now such a voluminous accumulation of evidence of the existence of flying saucers from outer space that we don't need to have a saucer land in each person's backyard to prove it to them. What we need is better dissemination of existing evidence. Through closer affiliation and [cooperation] this goal can be achieved."

This commentary was made forty years ago, but the same could be said today.

Was visitation from distant worlds taking place in the fifties?

That is a question that we are still contemplating today.

In the desert of southern California at a place called Giant Rock it seemed as though it was. George Van Tassel was not only being contacted with messages about saving the Earth but was also given plans for a structure that would reverse aging. That structure was called the Integratron. With donated funds and many years of labor the Integratron was built. Though it was never completed, the Integratron still stands alone in the desert as a monument to a man and an era of flying saucer contact.

George Van Tassel died suddenly on February 9, 1978, of a heart attack. With his death, an era came to a close. The Church of Universal Wisdom and the College of Universal Wisdom closed their doors. The wondrous flying saucer conventions at Giant Rock were no more.

In the seventeen years during which the conventions were held at Giant Rock nearly every notable in the flying saucer field attended: George Adamski, Daniel Fry, Truman Bethtrum, Gabriel Green, Frank Stranges, Howard Menger, Calvin Girvin, Robert Short, and many, many more. No other flying saucer event has ever garnered as much attention or had as large an attendance as the Giant Rock conventions.

George Adamski, another leading contactee of the era, was born in Poland on April 17, 1891. When he was two years old, his parents left Poland, and settled in Dunkirk, New York. His parents were deeply religious and encouraged George to explore spirituality.

Adamski was always disturbed by the fact that human beings could not seem to live in harmony. He felt that we were was so caught up in political power and competition that we ignored the universal laws of nature. Even before his contact with the space brothers, Adamski's goal in life was to teach universal peace and harmony.

Adamski's parents could not afford to provide him with a formal education, so he relied on self-study. In 1913 he joined the army. He served in the Thirteenth Cavalry on the Mexican border. His five years in the army reinforced his determination to find a way to create world harmony. He was honorably discharged in 1919.

On Christmas 1917 he married Mary Shimbersky. After his marriage Adamski traveled around the country for many years, taking any job that was available. During this time, he gathered a great deal of information about the problems and suffering of the common people.

When he was forty, Adamski moved to Laguna Beach, California, and devoted his life to teaching universal peace. As his popularity grew, he began to give lectures all over California.

During this time, one of Adamski's students gave him a telescope, and Adamski began to spend a great deal of time gazing at the heavens and taking pictures of the sky.

In 1940, just before the second World War, Adamski and several of his followers left Laguna Beach to settle in Valley Center, a small village along the road to Palomar Mountain. Here, during the war, he and his group established what they hoped would be a self-sustaining community called Palomar Gardens.

In 1944, Adamski sold the Valley Center ranch. He and his followers moved to a place 6 miles south of Palomar Mountain. They cleared an area and built living quarters and a small café, which was run by Alice K. Wells. He called this community Palomar Terraces.

At this time, Adamski bought a 15-inch telescope and built a small observatory. In 1946, during a meteor shower, he saw a large cigar-shaped ship in the sky. In 1947 he and his associates watched a group of spacecraft cross the sky. In 1953 he published *Flying Saucers Have Landed*. Then, in 1954, author Desmond Leslie came to Palomar to interview Adamski.

George Hunt Williamson, a disciple of Adamski's, was with him during his visit with the spacemen. Williamson and Adamski saw the first spacemen on November 20, 1952.

There were many leaders in the contactee movement but Van Tassel and Adamski were the charismatic stars of the era.

The Astar Command:

Location: Giant Rock, California

Witnesses: George Van Tassel
Beti King
Tuieta
Tuella (Thelma B. Terrell)

Encounter Type: Contact

Craft Type: Flying saucer

Alien Type: Human

Alien Characteristics: Although human in appearance, Astar is an "etheric" who lives on a higher vibratory level than humans. The physical descriptions of Astar vary, it seems, with each author. He is, according to different sources, just under 6 feet tall, or 7 feet tall. He has a fair complexion, or he is very dark. He has a hook nose or a nose that is not prominent.

Home World: Methaira, Alpha Centauri

Sources: *The Emergence of a Phenomenon: UFOs from the Beginning Through 1959*, by Jerome Clark; *High Strangeness: UFOs from 1960 Through 1979*, by Jerome Clark; *Psychic and UFO Revelations in the Last Days*, by Timothy Green Beckley; *The UFO Encyclopedia*, by Margaret Sachs; *The Encyclopedia of UFOs*, by Ronald Story; *I Rode a Flying Saucer*, by George Van Tassel.

Reliability: 2

Narrative: Astar, commandant of Quadra Sector, Patrol Section Schare, revealed his existence to George Van Tassel through psychic communications and channeling. Astar provided Van Tassel with a message suggesting that the development of atomic weapons threatened the existence of the planet and that if the work did not cease immediately, Astar would be forced to eliminate all projects connected with such research.

Much of the "writing" done by Astar suggested that Earth's population would be seriously reduced by the coming atomic war. In some cases it was suggested that the war would be cleansing. Today it seems that these types of warnings are interpreted as referring to natural disasters that will wipe out the majority of the population.

Astar has been channeled by a number of different contactees and was even photographed. The photograph, taken by an Italian, shows an androgynous figure that is identified as "Astar Sheran, Commander in Chief of the Extraplanetary Space Fleet."

Interestingly, Christian Fundamentalist Kelly L. Segraves warns that Astar and his followers are servants of the Antichrist. Others outside the contactee circle also warn that "fallen angels are . . . appearing unto man in the guise of visitors from other planets."

Astar's ship and apparently his command as well are in orbit 72,000 miles from Earth. Fleets of Etheria are also stationed within the Schare, and they represent what is called the Confederation of Planets for Peace. According to Tuella, "We are a branch of the greater Federation of Free Worlds which comprises the totality of

94

the Space Commands throughout the Omniverse. While my own administration is local to the Commands of this solar system, I am not restricted to this sector for my service, for I represent our system in the councils of other galaxies and universes throughout the vast cosmos."

The Domsten Contact:

DECEMBER 20, 1958

Location: Helsingbord, Sweden

Witnesses: Hans Gustafsson (age 25)
             Stig Rydberg (30)

Encounter Type: CE-III: contact

Craft Type: Disc

Alien Type: Nonhumanoid slugs

Alien Characteristics: These creatures were described as 4 feet long and about 14 inches wide, with no extremities. They were said to be lead-gray in color.

Home World: Unknown

Sources: *The Emergence of a Phenomenon: UFOs from the Beginning Through 1959,* by Jerome Clark; *Flying Saucers: The Startling Evidence of the Invasion from Outer Space,* by Coral Lorenzen; *APRO Bulletin,* January 1959.

Reliability: 0

Narrative: The two men were driving home just before 3:00 A.M. when they spotted a strange light off to their right. They stopped the car, got out, and walked toward a disc-shaped object.

In the field near the road they were attacked by lead-gray creatures with no arms or legs. They wrapped their bodies around the men and tried to drag them toward the disc.

Gustafsson was able to grab a pole so that the creatures couldn't drag him to the craft. Rydberg pushed the beings away from him, ran away, locked himself in the car, and began blowing the horn. Apparently that upset the creatures; they gave up the abduction attempt and returned to their craft.

There was an investigation. Favorable reports were sent to NICAP headquarters and to Coral Lorenzen at APRO. But problems arose. The men began telling their tale on the lecture circuit. Not long after that, they told an audience that they had seen another saucer land. This time, they said, they boarded it and took a ride into space. The occupants, unlike the gray slugs, were friendly.

Gustafsson and Rydberg were judged sane, but a psychologist, Michael Wachter, said that neither of the men seemed credible. In fact, more evidence that the story was a hoax was ignored by most researchers. Contradictory statements by the men, as well as the shifting nature of the contact, should have convinced researchers that there was nothing to the tale. Those clues were ignored, however, as were the later antics of the two men.

Both men died fairly young. In the 1980s Gustafsson's brother told researchers that his brother had admitted to him that the story was a hoax. An interview with Christian Johansen, who, as a fourteen-year-old, had sold tickets to one of the lectures, also said the case was a hoax. According to Johansen, the lecturers had told him and his mother that the story was an invention.

The Brooksville Robot:

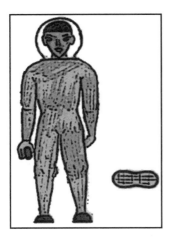

Location: Brooksville, Florida

Witnesses: John Reeves (age 66)

Encounter Type: CE-III: contact

Craft Type: Domed disc

Alien Type: Robotic

Alien Characteristics: The creature, which was about 5 feet tall, wore a one-piece silver suit topped by a glass bubble. It had smooth-looking tan skin. The eyes were slanted, far apart, and close to the ears. The chin was pointed.

Home World: Moniheya (Venus)

Sources: *The UFO Casebook,* by Kevin D. Randle; *High Strangeness: UFOs from 1960 Through 1979,* by Jerome Clark; *International UFO Reporter,* May–June 1995; *Encounters with UFO Occupants,* by Coral and Jim Lorenzen.

Reliability: 6   This is based on the reports of physical evidence being recovered and the footprints that were photographed. In many similar cases, there was no evidence offered at all.

Narrative: John Reeves, a retired longshoreman who lived on the outskirts of Brooksville, had trouble sleeping. He decided to take a walk, and in the woods behind his house he came upon an object—a domed disc 20 to 30 feet in diameter—that looked like nothing from this world. From the left came a robotlike creature; it was walking toward the craft. It stopped, turned, and raised something to its face, at eye level, almost like someone raising a camera. There was a bright flash, like a flash bulb, and then the robot continued walking and boarded the ship. The landing gear retracted, and the craft took off with a loud roar and a high-pitched whistle.

Unlike so many others who have claimed contact and said they had evidence, Reeves actually produced it. After the creature disappeared into the ship, Reeves found two sheets of paper that he claimed were left behind by the creature. He picked them up and showed them to local deputies, but the air force eventually took them for analysis. Reeves later claimed, and one of the deputy sheriffs confirmed, that the papers returned by the air force were not the same ones that had been taken from him.

UFO researcher Jerry Clark suggested that the analysis of those papers, which included the use of chemicals and various lights, not to mention the handling by the various interested parties, changed the chemical composition enough so that the returned papers didn't seem like the ones originally surrendered to the military. It must be noted, however, that Reeves did claim to have evidence and that he produced that evidence and surrendered it to the authorities. That put him ahead of almost everyone else who claimed to have seen alien creatures on other occasions.

Reeves, however, began to claim additional contacts with the other alien beings. He had meals with the alien creatures and then took flights with them to their home world. Although he suggested it was in another galaxy, it was, in fact, Venus, in our own solar system.

As a testament to his sighting, Reeves erected a monument in his yard with the intention of being buried under it. Reeves, however, had tax problems and lost his property. When the new owners took over, they demolished his monument.

The Andreasson Affair:

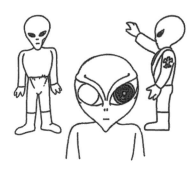

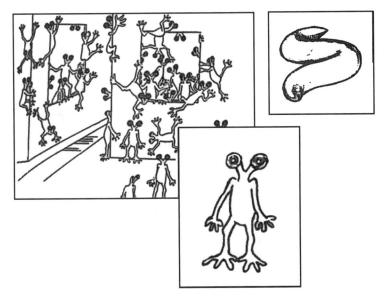

Location: South Ashburnham, Massachusetts

Witnesses: Betty Andreasson
              Waino Aho
              Eva Aho

Encounter Type: Abduction, contact

Craft Type: Oval-shaped saucer

Alien Type: Gray

Alien Characteristics: These aliens were small creatures with bald pear-shaped heads and large, slanted black eyes. They had three fingers on each hand. They were about 4 feet tall and were dressed in blue coveralls with the insignia of a bird on the sleeve. The leader of the group, though otherwise similar to the other creatures, had one white eye and one black eye.

Betty Andreasson also described a strange creature about 3 feet tall that had two arms and two legs but no head. Instead, they had eyes at the ends of two long stalks that could move independently. Andreasson said she saw these beings climbing all over the sides of buildings.

She also described a sluglike creature that was consumed by fire and then rose again as a big bird. When she first described this event, she was surprised to learn of the legend of the Phoenix.

Home World: The name of their home world, according to Andreasson, was unpronounceable; all she could say was that it began with a *Z* and contained lots of consonants.

Sources: *The Watchers*, by Raymond E. Fowler; *The Watchers II*, by Raymond E. Fowler; *The Andreasson Affair*, by Raymond E. Fowler; *The Andreasson Affair, Phase Two*, by Raymond E. Fowler; *High Strangeness: UFOs from 1960 Through 1979*, by Jerome Clark; *UFO Abductions: A Dangerous Game*, by Philip J. Klass; *Secret Life*, by David M. Jacobs.

Reliability: 2

Narrative: Betty Andreasson became aware of a pinkish light outside her house. Then a number of alien beings entered through a closed wooden door. When the beings entered the house, the other members of her family lapsed into some type of coma. As a devout Christian Fundamentalist, she thought at first that they might be angels. She soon realized that they weren't.

She and the leader of the group exchanged greetings, and she asked if they would like something to eat. She was told that her guests could only eat food that had been burned, but apparently that detail had lost something in the translation.

After the group leader made a comment, Andreasson was inspired to give him a copy of the family Bible. The leader, who identified himself as Quazgaa, handed her a thin blue book. Here, finally, was physical evidence that the event had taken place. But the thin blue book, possibly the most important piece of evidence to be received, has since disappeared. Andreasson seems to have misplaced it.

After this exchange, she was floated through the door and out toward the craft. Apparently Quazgaa sensed Andreasson's apprehension. Somehow the bottom of the saucer became transparent so that she could look inside. Once inside, she was subjected to a painful physical examination. She described the same needle-into-the-navel procedure discussed by Betty Hill a couple of years earlier, and she talked about a probe that was pushed up her nose.

Andreasson described being placed in a chair inside a plastic bubble that was then filled with a liquid. Air hoses were connected to her nose and mouth. During this time she was apparently taken to another world and given a message of peace and warning by the alien beings. She had been chosen to bring a message to the people of Earth. Part of the message was a warning that no one would believe her incredible tale until much later.

Eventually she was returned to her home. She had no memory of the events after seeing the lights in the backyard. Her father, who was staying with her at the time, recalled looking through the windows and seeing creatures that reminded him of Halloween freaks. They spotted him and he "felt kind of queer." That was all he remembered.

A few days after this event one of Andreasson's children, Becky, told her mother that she'd had a vivid dream about spacemen. Andreasson told her daughter that it had not been a dream; it had been real. To prove it, she showed Becky the thin blue book.

When questioned about the book under hypnosis on July 23, 1977, Andreasson seemed to be gripped by a paralysis that she associated with her abduction. She seemed to be speaking an unknown language, and the investigators believed that the aliens were somehow preventing her from speaking about the book. The idea is somewhat contradictory since she had been given the book by the leader of the expedition. Of course, as noted, she somehow lost this valuable piece of evidence.

It was during this hypnotic regression session that Andreasson began to channel—that is, another alien, Andantio, began speaking through her. The researchers attempted to question Andantio, but Raymond Fowler didn't know if they were actually speaking to an alien or to Andreasson's subconscious.

Under repeated hypnotic regressions, Andreasson began to tell of additional abductions beginning on August 7, 1944 (predating those claimed by Sara Shaw in the Tujunga Canyon abductions), when she was a small child. In 1949, Andreasson said, she met in the woods a humanoid creature that she would see again in her adult life. In 1961, again according to her, and just days after the Barney and Betty Hill abduction, she met a tall gray humanoid who gave her a "Christian-flavored message."

After the 1967 abduction, Andreasson became interested in UFOs and began reading about them. In the decade before she first underwent hypnotic regression, she had the opportunity to read a great deal about UFO abductions, including *The Interrupted Journey*, which told of Barney and Betty Hill, and, of course, to watch the NBC movie *The UFO Incident* about the Hill abduction, which had aired in October 1975. The fact that those narratives were available, however, does not mean that Andreasson read or saw them, only that the opportunity was there.

Hignon Encounter:

Location: North boundary of the Medicine Bow National Forest, Wyoming

Witnesses: Carl Hignon

Encounter Type: Abduction, contact

Alien Type: Humanoid

Alien Characteristics: The humanoid was over 6 feet tall and weighed, according to Hignon's estimate, about 180 pounds. The skin tone was like that of an Oriental, and the face seemed to blend into the neck. The creature was dressed in a one-piece suit like that of a scuba diver. The metal belt had a six-pointed star in the middle.

Home World: Unknown

Sources: *APRO Bulletin,* March 1975; *High Strangeness: UFOs from 1960 Through 1979,* by Jerome Clark; *Encounters with UFO Occupants,* by Coral Lorenzen; *Abducted,* by Coral and Jim Lorenzen; *The UFO Encyclopedia,* by John Spencer; *The Encyclopedia of UFOs,* by Ronald D. Story.

Reliability: 2

Narrative: Carl Hignon, an oil-field driller, supplemented his income by hunting in the Wyoming countryside. On one such expedition, Hignon saw five elk standing together. He raised his rifle and fired, but he felt no kick from the high-powered weapon. The bullet, according to Hignon, seemed to float from the barrel and fall to the ground 50 feet from him. There was no report as he fired. In fact, there was no sound from anything around him.

Hearing a twig snap, Hignon turned and saw a humanoid standing near him. It was over 6 feet tall and weighed about 180 pounds. The skin tone was like that of an Oriental, and the face seemed to blend into the neck. Like so many others, Hignon said that the creature was dressed in a one-piece suit that reminded him of a scuba diving suit. The metal belt had a six-pointed star in the middle.

The first thing the creature asked was "How you doin'?"

Hignon said, "Pretty good."

He was then asked if he was hungry, but before he could answer, a small package floated toward him. Inside were four pills. He was told they would last for four days. He took one of the pills and put the other three into a pocket.

In the distance, Hignon spotted what he believed to be the creature's ship. It looked like a box with no landing gear, no hatches, no other exterior features. The creature, realizing that Hignon had seen the ship, asked if he would like to take a ride.

Before he could answer, he found himself in the ship. It took off, and soon Hignon found himself on a planet "163,000 light-miles" from Earth. From inside the ship, he was able to see buildings on the alien planet. One of them he described as looking like the Space Needle. It was surrounded by intense rotating spotlights.

Hignon threw up his hands, shouting that the lights were hurting his eyes. They were burning him.

One of the aliens responded, "Your sun burns us."

The next thing Hignon remembered was walking down the road, feeling confused. He still had his rifle, but he didn't know who he was or where he was. In the distance he saw a truck parked in a stand of trees. He decided to use it for shelter, not realizing that it was his own vehicle.

As he sat in the truck, confused, dazed, and cold, he heard a voice on the two-way radio. He unhooked the microphone from the dashboard and called for help. By staying in constant communication, he was able to assist the searchers in their attempts to find him.

Once he'd been found, his family was alerted, and they joined him at the hospital. Still disoriented, he kept asking for the pills given to him by the alien. It wasn't until late the next day that he began to regain his memory and equilibrium. He was released from the hospital and told to get some rest.

Dr. Leo Sprinkle interviewed Hignon and conducted a number of hypnotic regression sessions. Under hypnosis, Hignon provided more details, telling Sprinkle that the name of the alien leader was Ausso One. Hignon also learned more about the trip to Ausso One's home world.

There was one piece of corroborating evidence: the bullet fired by Hignon at the beginning of his adventure. Hignon had located it and put it into his canteen pouch, where he later found it. He couldn't easily identify it and took it to the Carbon County Sheriff's Office. There it was identified as having come from a 7mm Magnum rifle. The deputy who examined it said it looked as if it had been turned inside out. He couldn't explain the condition. The bullet was given to Walter Walker, formerly an APRO scientific consultant, for examination. Later it was turned over to Sprinkle. In 1994, Sprinkle told Randle that the bullet had disappeared.

What is interesting about the Hignon case is that it parallels more closely the tales of contact told by Dan Fry, George Adamski, and George Van Tassel than it does the abduction reports. Hignon was not forced on board and was given a view of another world. Although he was examined, he didn't describe any of the invasive procedures mentioned by abductees. Hignon had the opportunity to "chat" with the aliens, whereas most abductees suggest that any discussion is the result of the aliens' attempts to gain information about human life.

Given that, however, many of those who would have rejected, out of hand, most contactees' tales have accepted Hignon's. They have said that those who have interviewed him find him to be a sincere, seemingly honest man who had a strange adventure. Of course, they also point to the physical evidence and the fact that others saw strange lights on the night Hignon was abducted. These observations seem to suggest that the Hignon tale, unlike those of the contactees, is authentic.

The Billy Meier Contacts:

JANUARY 28, 1975

Location: Hinwill, Switzerland

Witnesses: Billy Meier

Encounter Type: Contact

Craft Type: Disc-shaped beam ship

Alien Type: Human

Alien Characteristics: This alien was very human-looking with pale skin.

Home World: Erra, in the Pleiades

Sources: *Light Years,* by Gary Kinder; *High Strangeness: UFOs from 1960 Through 1979,* by Jerome Clark.

Reliability: 0

Narrative: Although Eduard "Billy" Meier claimed to have sighted many UFOs dating back to his childhood and to have had mental contact with the alien creatures, it wasn't until 1975 that they landed and he met with them in person. After photographing a craft that had flown nearby, Meier was surprised when it landed in a nearby meadow. To his surprise, a beautiful pale-skinned amber-haired woman left the craft and walked over to Meier.

Semjase (Sem-Ya-See) told Meier she was from an extraterrestrial civilization that had originated thousands of years earlier on a planet in the constellation Lyra. (It is interesting to note that all these space travelers refer to their home systems using constellation names that were coined on Earth.) They had come to Earth and found it so idyllic that they had educated the primitive humans and intermarried with them. After this first wave was wiped out in a war, a second wave landed and was also destroyed in war. Semjase was part of the third wave of aliens who communicated through telepathy and revealed themselves to selected humans.

Semjase provided proof of her claims for Meier. The aliens would make their beam ships visible to him, and he was to photograph as many of them as possible. The results were spectacular. Books have been devoted to the photographs that Meier took.

But Meier didn't just photograph the ships. On July 17, 1975, he was able to photograph, from inside one of the ships, the linking of American and Soviet spacecraft. Here was a first: one of the contactees had been allowed to take pictures from space of an event that had been recorded by news organizations from around the world. (Critics would suggest, however, that Meier had put the photographs together through trick photography and the use of footage from NASA.)

Unlike many flying saucers, the beam ships were able to travel through time, and Meier was able to photograph dinosaurs, a caveman, and even an earthquake in San Francisco.

The evidence offered by Meier, however, has been less than persuasive. The photographs have been challenged by experts who suggest trickery. Some investigators have even discovered the strings used to hold the miniature ships aloft. Model spacecraft have been found in Meier's barn, though he claims that the models were simply inspired by the real ships.

Meier remains in contact with the alien creatures. His photographs, books, and videotapes are now sold around the world. His stature, in fact, is greater than that once enjoyed by George Adamski and George Van Tassel.

Part III

The Abductees

The concept of general human interaction, as a contactee or an abductee, with alien beings is not one that is easily accepted. Although tales of contact were told at the beginning of the UFO phenomenon, they were not accepted by mainstream ufology. Contactees told tales of meetings with benevolent space brothers who provided messages of peace, who flew the lucky few to planets inside and outside the solar system, and who promised worldwide prosperity. The contactees, however, failed to provide any evidence that they traveled to other star systems or even that they met the aliens.

The perception changed with the abduction phenomenon. These people were not contacted by kind aliens who worried only about human progress but were accosted by beings who cared nothing for human emotions or physical health. The aliens gathered their data dispassionately and then returned the humans to their own environment with little thought to the trauma caused by the abduction.

Ever since the Barney and Betty Hill abduction was first reported in the mid-1960s, hundreds, if not thousands or even millions, have claimed similar experiences. In 1992, Las Vegas businessman Robert Bigelow commissioned the Roper Organization to study the abduction phenomenon. Although the results are open to interpretation, they seem to suggest that as many as three million Americans have had experiences that suggest an abduction at some point in their lives.

Ufological research in other areas slowed as more investigators began to study abduction. Resources that might have helped provide answers to the many questions about extraterrestrial visitation were sucked into abduction research. Reports, studies, and investigations claimed many things about the aliens, their experimentation on board the flying saucers, and their motives. Thousands of abductees have been interviewed using a variety of techniques including hypnotic regression. In the end, however, nothing substantial was found. As in the contactee phenomenon of the 1950s, the abductees and the researchers failed to provide any evidence they had met the aliens. We had only the eyewitnesses' testimony and the suspect corroboration of other abductees from around the country.

Contrary to popular belief, the first abduction report was not made by Barney and Betty Hill in 1961, nor was it provided by Antonio Villas-Boas in 1957. The first recorded abduction might have been the Great Airship sightings in the late nineteenth century: Colonel H. G. Shaw, apparently a former member of the staff of the *Stockton* (California) *Evening Mail,* said that he and a companion, Camille Spooner, were leaving Lodi, California, on horseback in the early evening of November 25, 1896, "when the horse stopped suddenly and gave a snort of terror."

Shaw claimed that he saw three figures who stood nearly 7 feet tall and were very thin. They looked human and didn't seem to be hostile, so Shaw tried to communicate with them. According to Shaw, they didn't understand him and responded by "warbling" in a chantlike monotone.

Shaw continued his description: "They were without any sort of clothing, but were covered with a natural growth as soft as silk to the touch and their skin was like velvet. Their faces and heads were without hair, the ears were very small, and the nose had the appearance of polished ivory, while the eyes were large and lustrous. The mouth, however, was small and it seemed . . . they were without teeth."

Shaw also said they had small nailless hands and long narrow feet. By touching one, he discovered that the beings were nearly weightless. Shaw said he believed they weighed less than an ounce.

They tried to "lift me," he said, "probably with the intention of carrying me away." When they couldn't budge either Shaw or his companion, they gave up. They then flashed lights at a nearby bridge where a large airship was hovering. They walked toward the craft using a swaying motion and touching the ground only every 15 feet or so. Then, according to Shaw, "With a little spring they rose to the machine, opened a door in the side and disappeared."

Two days later John A. Horen claimed that he had met a stranger who took him to an airship. He and the stranger boarded the ship, toured southern California, and then flew to Hawaii. Horen's wife laughed at the tale, said that he was well known as a habitual practical joker and that he had been asleep next to her that night.

A week or so later, in early December 1896, two California fishermen, Giuseppe Valinziano and Luigi Valdivia, said they had been held on the airship for a number of hours while the crew made repairs. The "captain" of the craft would provide only vague clues about the origin of the ship but did say its invention would be announced to the world within weeks. And as is so often the case in these stories, the details are also vague.

It would be nearly twenty years before another abduction was reported. In August 1915 near Gallipoli, Turkey, a British regiment was formed to climb a hill near Suvla Bay. As the soldiers began to move, they saw six to eight clouds hovering near the hill. One of the clouds slowly descended until it was resting on the ground.

Men of a New Zealand regiment watched as the British soldiers marched into the cloud. When the last of the soldiers had entered, the cloud began to lift. The British soldiers were never seen again, according to the tale.

At the war's end, British government officials demanded to know what had happened to the missing regiment. Turkey denied that they had captured an entire regiment or had even fought the regiment.

Another apparent abduction attempt was reported within a month of the Kenneth Arnold sighting in 1947. On July 23, Jose Higgins was with a number of fellow workers near Bauru, Brazil, when they witnessed the landing of a large flying saucer. Higgins remained behind after his fellow workers fled in terror. He was confronted by creatures 7 feet tall with round bald heads, huge eyes, and long legs.

Although Higgins found the creatures strangely attractive, when they attempted to lure him into the saucer, he ran. He hid in the bushes and watched the creatures spend an hour leaping and jumping around. They stopped long enough to draw what Higgins believed was a map of the solar system indicating they came from Uranus. When they finished playing, they returned to the ship and took off.

Another case of apparent abduction that hinted at some of the more sinister aspects of the phenomenon was reported in the *Flying Saucer Review*. An unidentified Frenchwoman said that she had been hurrying home to prepare dinner on May 20, 1950, at about four o'clock in the afternoon, when she suddenly found herself inside a brilliant, blinding light. She felt paralyzed when first touched by the bright light. Although she had been alone on the path and had seen no one around her, two huge black hands appeared in front of her.

The woman said the hands grabbed her from above in much the way talons of a bird of prey would. As the hands touched her, she felt an electrical shock, and she felt completely helpless and without reflexes. Her head was jerked back hard against a cold iron chest. She felt the cold through her hair and on the back of her neck. The hands were also cold, and she wasn't sure they were made of flesh. Big fingers seemed to choke off her screams and pinch her nose so that she couldn't breathe. She was now at the mercy of the being.

She was then pulled from the path and through bushes to a small pasture. She tried to call for help, but she had no voice; her cry was nothing but a tiny shrill cry.

The attack stopped as abruptly as it had begun. The hand gradually slipped away from her face. Eventually she was able to sit up and finally to stand. When she heard noise to her left, in the bushes, she thought she would see her aggressor, but she saw nothing.

Terrified, she stumbled back to the path to seek help. She felt nervous and exhausted, and she had a strange metallic taste in her mouth. Her back hurt, as if she had been burned.

After several minutes she reached a turn in the path and could see several houses. But before she could reach them, she heard a great noise, "like a violent windstorm." The trees, according to the woman, were bending as if in a "sudden storm." There was a bright white light, but she saw nothing behind the light or in the sky near it.

She reached the house of a man identified only as the "lock-keeper" and opened the door. Those inside rushed to her and asked what had happened. They too had seen the light. They told her they could see red marks on her face, looking like large red bars.

Interestingly, the night before, the same woman had seen what she thought was a shooting star. But instead of falling to the ground or burning itself out, it stopped, then climbed until it seemed to join the other stars. It grew larger, swung back and forth, and blinked on and off. It disappeared suddenly, curving upward at a great rate of speed.

During an official investigation of the attempted abduction, the investigators got nowhere, and the case was dropped. However, it is reportedly still regarded as an unsolved abduction. This tale provided hints of what was to come.

It wasn't until 1957 that there was a report that could be considered the first of the alien abductions. Antonio Villas-Boas (see "Antonio Villas-Boas: October 15, 1957," page 133), a South American farmer, told UFO researcher Dr. Olavo Fontes that he was dragged into a flying saucer. His story became the prototypical abduction report. All of the later tales, including that of Barney and Betty Hill (see "The Hill Abduction: September 19, 1961," page 142), the first Americans to receive publicity surrounding their claims, mirrored the groundbreaking story of Villas-Boas.

John Fuller's book, *The Interrupted Journey,* told the Hill tale and launched the abduction phenomenon. But even after the Hill story was reported nationally, few additional reports surfaced.

Although American researchers were now aware of the Villas-Boas and Hill cases, it would be a number of years before another solid report would emerge. On December 3, 1967, Patrolman Herbert Schirmer was driving on the outskirts of Ashland, Nebraska, when he was abducted. Like so many others, he had no memory of the event until he underwent hypnotic regression.

Interestingly, each of these three cases represented a different aspect of the abduction phenomenon. Villas-Boas remembered the abduction consciously, the Hills remembered a UFO sighting but not the abduction itself. Betty Hill later had dreams about her abduction. Schirmer remembered a sighting but recalled the abduction only under hypnosis; he had no dreams about it. This provides some clues to the abduction phenomenon that should be considered here.

Villas-Boas, because he remembered without memory enhancing techniques, provides abduction researchers with the ammunition needed to refute the many skeptics. Here was a tale of abduction that was not suppressed by the aliens nor was it repressed by the victim. There could be no question that it was not a mentally induced delusion created in the moments between waking and sleep. Villas-Boas, because he was outdoors on his tractor, did not experience sleep paralysis. And he could not have been influenced by a hypnotherapist, because he was not hypnotized to tell his tale. His was, it might be said, a pure experience.

The same cannot be said of the Hill abduction. Neither Barney nor Betty had any conscious memory of the event. Betty Hill, within days of their UFO sighting, wanted to use hypnosis to recover possible hidden memories. During those first few days she was consumed by the tale and a belief that aliens were involved, and she began to dream about abduction. She had no conscious memory of it, but her subconscious began to warn her of that possibility. At least that is the theory presented by the many UFO investigators who have studied the case.

Abduction researchers today would have us believe that dreams are actual experiences that have been mistaken for fantasy. Through the use of hypnosis, many abductees, including the Hills, were taught that their dreams were memories of actual experiences because "the dream was so vivid." Betty Hill, for example, remarked that she was astounded by how vivid her dreams were.

Abduction researchers also suggested that these people are dreaming about aliens because they were actually abducted. The victims don't realize that thinking about aliens and abductions in the daytime increases the likelihood of dreaming about them at night. In fact, we all dream about the things we experience and think about during the day. This phenomenon is called "day residue" by dream researchers. A majority of abductees have sleep disturbances, which in many cases increases dream recall and causes dream material to become more bizarre. Many abductees also have vivid nightmares.

For most of us, a dream is immediately recognized as such. But before the age of five, we cannot tell the difference between reality, dreams, and fantasy. We see our dreams as real, and we become terrified of the monsters we see on television. By the time we reach school age, however, we can recognize the difference

124

between reality, dreams, and fantasies. As adults we are able to catalog memories of dreams as separate from memories of reality. For some these distinctions may remain unclear, however. Some people can never form boundaries between dreams and reality. For them, reality has a ruffled edge rather than a clear boundary.

When boundaries fail to form, it becomes difficult for the person to tell what is real and what is not. To the person with boundary problems, REM dreams become reminiscence, and what has been imagined is interpreted as actual experience. The boundary-impaired make statements like "I don't know if I dreamed this or if it really happened."

It is important to note that alien-abduction dreams revolve around themes of boundary violation. The dreams of abduction and medical experiments become both a metaphor for the early violations and a vehicle to express the feeling of helpless violation. For an "abductee" with poor boundaries, dreams may become the vehicle that leads them into a life of endless therapy and constantly increasing dreams of abduction. As the dreams inevitably increase in frequency, the person becomes more and more convinced that they are real and that they are escalating. Soon the dreams become indistinguishable from actual experience; fantasy thrusts its way into reality.

It is important, however, that both Barney and Betty Hill consciously remembered seeing the UFO along the highway. As they drove, they argued over the identity of the object. They stopped so they could see it better, and at one point Barney left the car with binoculars and returned convinced that they would be captured.

According to Fuller, writing in *The Interrupted Journey,* "Some ten days after the sighting, Betty began having a series of vivid dreams. They continued for five successive nights. Never in her memory has she recalled dreams of such detail and intensity. They dominated her waking life during that week and continued to plague her afterward. . . . When eventually she did mention rather casually that she was having a series of nightmares, Barney was sympathetic."

Fuller continued, "Realizing that Barney was attempting to put the UFO event out his mind, Betty refrained from discussing the nightmares with him. But she began telling a few close friends, one of whom, a fellow social worker, urged her to write down her dreams."

These discussions reinforce the triggering mechanism for a belief in alien abduction. Initially, Betty Hill had no conscious memory of the actual abduction; the information came to her exclusively through dreams. So once again we find a number of researchers accepting dreams as reality, although there is no reason to believe that Betty Hill's dreams reflected reality.

Later, under hypnosis with Dr. Benjamin Simon, both Barney and Betty Hill, with sufficient emotion to impress researchers, told the tale of their abduction. But it should be understood that Dr. Simon was interested only in treating the psychological problems of his patients. The introduction that Simon provided to *The Interrupted Journey* gives no indication that he believed the abduction tales as told by Betty Hill and originally "remembered" in her dreams.

The Hills underwent hypnosis to recover their memory of the abduction, though it can be and has been argued that the memories were inspired by Betty Hill's dreams. Herbert Schirmer, on the other hand, had no dreams. He recovered his memory of the abduction during hypnotic regression.

Hypnosis, according to many abduction researchers, is the only key available to unlock memories. Many retrieve their memories first under hypnosis. Schirmer, for example, had no conscious memory of the abduction. The Allagash Four (See "The Allagash Abductions, August 20, 1976," page 189)—four men who were camping together in an isolated area of Maine—remembered a UFO sighting but nothing about alien abduction until they dreamed about it and then were hypnotized.

Thousands of abductions have been reported in recent decades. The witnesses now claim that in some instances the abductions began generations earlier. They say the aliens have been watching them, monitoring them, and tracking them since the turn of the century. The theory is that the aliens are conducting some huge and extensive research project.

The problem is that there is little or no physical evidence to support these claims. We have testimony from the victims of abduction, and we can see the trauma that has been inflicted, but little corroborative evidence exists. We are forced to look at the scars that some claim are the result of the abduction, but that is of little value. The evidence just isn't there to support the claims of alien abduction.

Yet these tales are being told by honest individuals. There is no doubt that most of them are relating, as accurately as they can, events they believe to have occurred. The researchers, for the most part, are as honest as the witnesses. They truly believe that they are gathering information that is important to the understanding of one aspect of the UFO phenomenon.

As in so many other areas of ufology, we still lack the evidence we need to prove that aliens from other planets are visiting Earth.

The Tujunga Canyon Abduction:

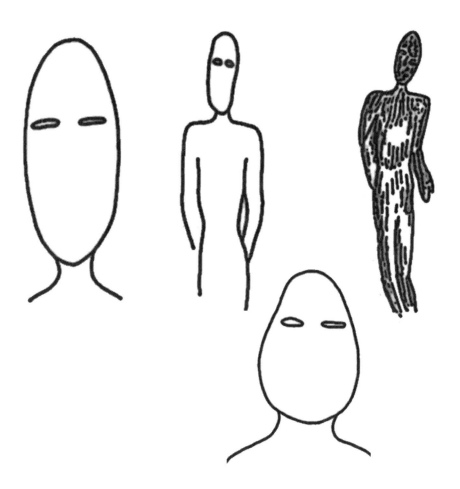

Location: Tujunga Canyon, California

Witnesses: Sara Shaw (pseudonym, age 21)
Jan Whitley (pseudonym, age 22)

Encounter Type: Abduction

Craft Type: Saturn-shaped disc

Alien Type: Humanoid

Alien Characteristics: These creatures originally described as black were very slender, with narrow shoulders and no facial features as if wearing ski masks. Only the eyes were visible. In later illustrations, the creatures are no longer black but are white without facial features.

Home World: Unknown

Sources: *The Tujunga Canyon Contacts*, by Ann Druffel and D. Scott Rogo; *World Atlas of UFO Sightings*, by John Spencer.

Reliability: 1

Narrative: Awakened by a bright light that she first thought was from motorcycle headlights, Sara Shaw watched as the glow swept back and forth in her yard, creating dancing shadows on her wall. When she quickly realized that the light was not from motorcycles, she checked the time and saw that it wasn't the sun about to rise. Her friend, Jan Whitley, also awakened by the lights, walked to the closet to get a robe.

An instant later Shaw again looked at the clock and saw that twenty minutes had passed. She told Whitley she had been standing at the closet door for more than twenty minutes, then realized she had read the clock wrong: two hours and twenty minutes had passed. Instead of kneeling on her pillows, looking out the window, as she had been, she was now seated on the bed. She knew that something strange and terrible had happened.

More than twenty years later, after watching a series of reports on UFOs, Shaw called UFO researcher Ann Druffel, hoping she could help her learn what had happened so long ago. With Druffel's help, Shaw underwent hypnotic regression and was able to recall the strange events.

She finally remembered that, while looking out the window, she had seen a group of people walking through the yard toward the house. The people entered the house, and apparently Jan Whitley struggled with them while Shaw was held to one side, fascinated by the fight.

Later Sara Shaw was inside a huge craft, or perhaps a domed room. Her roommate was struggling, and Shaw saw that the beings were trying to take off Jan Whitley's pajama top while Jan tried to get them to leave her alone.

The next thing Shaw remembered was being suspended over a table and undergoing a physical examination. First the aliens used some sort of machine, and then they examined her with their hands. During the examination, the aliens seemed interested in an old surgical scar.

During the examination, Shaw felt that she had been "numbered" with an invisible number four. Researchers speculated that this might have been a tracking method of some kind.

When the examination was over, Sara Shaw and Jan Whitley were floated back to the house. The alien beings then told her that she would remember nothing of the session on board the craft. She would forget all that had happened to her.

Investigators realized they needed to corroborate the tale, and Jan Whitley was the obvious source for the corroboration. Whitley did remember the conscious aspect of the abduction, just as Shaw had. And she mentioned that in 1956 she began to have vivid dreams, nightmares really, that were so real they didn't seem like dreams at all. They seemed to focus on an abductionlike scenario and alien creatures.

Whitley's friend, Emily Cronin, also recalled strange events. She and Jan Whitley described what might have been another abduction in 1956, one that didn't involve Shaw.

Cronin and Whitley were driving home and had pulled into a rest stop when they were confronted by a yellowish white light. Both women were paralyzed. Cronin later told investigators that she had the impression of a man watching them through the back window of the car. By concentrating, she was able to move one finger, and then the paralysis broke.

When asked if she'd had other similar experiences, Jan Whitley said that in 1967 or 1968 she had awakened unable to move. She said that ugly little faces were floating around the room above her. She felt as she had in the cabin in March 1953 during the abduction that was reported by Shaw.

What we have here, then, is a history of abductions that might have begun in 1953, though Whitley claimed to have seen her first UFO in the early 1940s. Like many others who claim abduction, she recovered her memory of the actual experience under hypnotic regression which provided rich detail. Because it was a dual abduction, it has been suggested that there is corroboration for this report. How could two people have the same delusion?

There is nothing in the backgrounds of any of these three women to suggest that they are lying. They sincerely believe that abductions took place. And like many of the others, they seem to have been the victims of repeated abductions. Their tales are not significantly different from those told by others.

It should be noted, however, that the Shaw-Whitley case did not come to the attention of investigators until after the airing of the TV movie about the Barney and Betty Hill abduction. Shaw claims that she never saw the film or read the book about the case. She had no interest in UFOs until she happened to see some local television reports and called for help.

Because it was claimed that this case took place in March 1953, it has been suggested it was the first real abduction. However, it was not reported until twenty years after the fact and more than a decade after the Hill case. By the time the investigation began, dozens of abduction cases had been reported in the popular press. Now, however, abductees are claiming even earlier abductions, beginning in the 1930s and 1940s. Yet the bottom line here is that the first reported abduction was that of Antonio Villas-Boas.

Antonio Villas-Boas:

Location: São Francisco de Salles, Minas Gerais, Brazil

Witnesses: Antonio Villas-Boas

Encounter Type: Abduction

Craft Type: Egg-shaped

Alien Type: Humanoid, more human than alien

Alien Characteristics: The beings wore helmets that hid everything except their eyes, which were protected by round glasses like the lenses in ordinary spectacles. Their eyes seemed to be much smaller than human eyes, though the witness believed that might have been the effect of the lenses. All of the aliens had light-colored eyes that appeared to be blue.

Home World: Unknown

Sources: *The October Scenario*, by Kevin Randle; *Encounters with UFO Occupants*, by Coral and Jim Lorenzen; *High Strangeness: UFOs from 1960 Through 1979*, by Jerome Clark; *UFO: The Com-*

plete Sightings, by Peter Brookesmith; *The Encyclopedia of UFOs,* edited by Ronald D. Story.

Reliability: 6

Narrative: The first case of alien abduction, as such, was reported on February 22, 1958, by Antonio Villas-Boas, a Brazilian farmer. He was interviewed by the Brazil representative of the Aerial Phenomena Research Organization (APRO), Dr. Olavo Fontes, and by a newspaper columnist, João Martins.

This case would become the model for abductions reported for the next twenty years. The point that must be made is that Villas-Boas couldn't have read about other abductions and then designed his story to follow those leads. Nor could Fontes have subtly guided him, because there had been no other abduction reports in the ufological literature. In 1957 this case was unique.

According to Villas-Boas, "It all began on the night of October 5, 1957." Villas-Boas had retired to his room after a party. Because of the heat, he opened the window. Outside, over a corral, he could see a bright fluorescent light. It seemed to sweep upward into the night sky, but there was no object behind the light. He called out to his brother, João, who refused to get up to look.

Villas-Boas then lay down, but soon got up again. The light was still there, and as he watched, it began to move toward the window. Villas-Boas slammed the shutters closed, but the light bled through the slats. He later told Fontes that he and his brother "watched the light appear through the crevices of our shutters . . . and shine through the tiles of the roof, lighting up the darkness of our room."

A few days later, on October 14, Villas-Boas was in one of the farm fields late at night with another brother. They saw a light so bright that it hurt their eyes. This time he tried to approach the light, which was hovering in the sky. As he approached it, the light moved off, evading him. He chased it from field to field until he grew tired.

The next night, October 15, 1957, Villas-Boas was plowing the fields late. At one o'clock on the morning of October 16, he noticed an extremely bright red star overhead. As he watched it, he saw that it was moving and growing larger as it approached him. He hesitated, wondering what to do, and in those few seconds the light became distinguishable as an egg-shaped craft descending toward his freshly plowed field. It came to a hover over him, its light so bright that Villas-Boas could no longer see his own tractor headlights.

Villas-Boas thought of trying to drive away, but the tractor had no real speed, and the object could easily overtake him. Running through the plowed field would be difficult, and if he stepped in a hole, he could break his leg. Escape seemed impossible.

A bright light seemed to come from the front of the craft that looked like an elongated egg. There were purple lights near the large red one, and there was a small red light on a flattened cupola on top of the ship that spun rapidly. As the object slipped toward the ground, three telescoping legs slid from beneath it.

Villas-Boas realized that the legs, like those of a camera tripod, were for landing. He turned his tractor around and stepped on the accelerator. Before he had driven far, however, the engine sputtered and died and the headlights faded out. He tried to restart it, but the ignition didn't work. He then opened the door on the side away from the alien craft, got out, and tried to run.

He had taken only a few steps when something touched his arm. He spun around and faced a short creature. Struggling to escape, he put a hand on the creature's chest and pushed. The alien being stumbled back and fell. But three other creatures grabbed Villas-Boas and lifted him. He twisted, kicked, and jerked with his arms. He shouted for help, but the beings held him tightly, moving slowly toward the craft.

A door opened in the ship, and a narrow ladder extended to the ground. The aliens tried to lift Villas-Boas into the ship, but he grabbed at the narrow railing and held on. One of the creatures peeled his fingers away from the flexible metal, and he was forced upward and through the door.

He found himself in a room with a metal rod running from the floor to the ceiling; he thought it supported the roof. The room itself was square, with polished silvery metal walls. To one side was an oddly shaped table surrounded by backless chairs.

For several minutes Villas-Boas and the aliens stood in the room. The creatures talked among themselves in a series of low, growling sounds while they held on to Villas-Boas. Eventually they stripped off his clothes, taking care not to rip anything. When he was naked, one of the aliens "washed" him with an oily-looking liquid that made him shiver as it dried.

Villas-Boas provided a description of the alien beings. While it is detailed as to what they wore, it provided few clues to what they actually looked like. He indicated that they were all small, no more than 5 feet tall. He said, during his long interview with Dr. Fontes, "I must declare that up to that moment I hadn't the slightest idea as to how those weird men looked nor what their features were like. All five of them wore a very tight-fitting siren suit made of soft, thick, unevenly striped gray material. This garment reached right up their necks where it was joined to a kind of helmet made of a gray material . . . that looked stiffer and was strengthened back and front by thin metal plates, one of which was three-cornered, at nose level. Their helmets hid everything except their eyes, which were protected by two round glasses, like the lenses in ordinary glasses. Through them, the men looked at me, and their eyes seemed to be much smaller than ours, though I believe that may have been the effect of the lenses. All of them had light-colored eyes that looked blue to me, but this I cannot vouch for."

He went on to describe their large helmets from which three tubes extended downward into the suit. He saw no evidence of any type of tank, and when asked about it, he had no explanation for the system of tubes or the lack of tanks.

He was forced deeper into the ship, into a smaller room where

137

blood samples were taken from under his chin by two figures holding two rubbery-looking pipes. After the samples were taken, he was left alone for an hour or more, sitting on a large couch. Then, feeling tired, he lay down, and then he noticed a strange odor in the room. From the walls, about head high, he saw gray smoke pouring into the room. Its thick, oily odor made him physically ill. He fought the feeling for several minutes but finally vomited.

Feeling better, Villas-Boas sat back on the couch, waiting. Eventually there was a noise at the door and he turned to see a woman entering. Like Villas-Boas, she was completely naked. She moved slowly, walked toward him, and embraced him, rubbing herself against his body.

The woman was short, reaching only up to his chin. Her light hair was almost white and looked as if it had been bleached heavily. In *Flying Saucer Occupants,* Coral Lorenzen wrote that the woman had blood-red hair under her arms. Lorenzen told Randle in a 1972 interview that she had changed that part of the testimony because she didn't want to mention the woman's red pubic hair.

The woman had slanted blue eyes that gave her an Arabian look. Her face was wide with high cheekbones, but her chin was very pointed, giving her whole face an angular look. She was slim, with high, very pointed breasts. Her stomach was flat, and her thighs were large. Her hands were small, but they looked like normal human hands.

The woman caressed him, showing him exactly what she wanted. Given the circumstances, Villas-Boas was surprised that he could respond at all, but he felt sexually excited. Later he suggested that his arousal was induced, perhaps by the liquid that had been rubbed on him.

She kept rubbing him, caressing his body, and in moments they were together on the couch. Villas-Boas responded to her, and before he realized what was happening, they were joined. According to him, she responded like a human woman.

When they finished, they stayed on the couch, petting, and in minutes, both were ready again. He tried to kiss her, but she refused, preferring to nibble his chin. After the second sex act, she avoided him. As she stood up, the door opened. One of the alien men stepped in and called to the woman. Before she left, she smiled at Villas-Boas, pointed to her stomach and then to the sky—"Southward," according to Villas-Boas.

One of the men came back and handed Villas-Boas his clothes. While dressing, he noticed that his cigarette lighter was missing. He thought he might have lost it during the struggle in the field or that it might have disappeared on the ship.

The creature directed him out of the small room and into another, where crew members were sitting, talking—or rather growling—among themselves. He was left out of the discussion, the aliens ignoring him, so he tried to fix the details of the room in his mind. On a table near the beings was a square box with a glass lid and a clocklike face. Thinking that he would need proof of his experience, he tried to steal it. Almost before he could move, one of the creatures jumped toward him and pushed him away.

At last one of the aliens motioned for him to follow. None of the others looked up as he was given a quick tour of the ship. The door was open again, with the ladder extending to the ground, but he and his escort didn't descend. Instead, they stepped onto a platform that went around the ship. Slowly they walked along it as the alien pointed out various features. Since he didn't speak, Villas-Boas didn't know the purpose of any of the things he was shown, including several machines with purplish lights. He glanced up at the cupola, which now emitted a greenish light and made a noise like a vacuum cleaner as it slowly spun.

When the tour ended, he was taken back to the ladder, and the alien motioned toward the ground. When Villas-Boas was at the bottom, he stopped and looked back, but the alien hadn't moved. Instead, he pointed to himself, then to the ground, and finally toward the sky. He signaled Villas-Boas to step back as he disappeared inside.

The ladder telescoped back into the craft, and when the door closed, there was no sign of a seam or a crack. The lights brightened, those on the cupola began to spin faster and faster, and the ship lifted quietly into the night sky.

As it disappeared, Villas-Boas walked back to his tractor. It was 5:30 A.M. He had been on the ship for more than four hours.

Villas-Boas told his mother about the encounter, but he didn't tell anyone else until February 1958. After reading several articles about flying saucers in *O Cruzeiro,* a Brazilian publication, he wrote to the author, João Martins. He also carved a model of the UFO and sent it to Martins. Not long after that, Martins arranged for Villas-Boas to be brought to Rio de Janeiro, where he and Dr. Fontes interviewed Villas-Boas, who produced a sworn statement.

Both men were impressed with Villas-Boas. He was a sincere, intelligent young man, who would eventually become an attorney. Martins, however, thought the story was too strange for *O Cruzeiro.* The only evidence of the tale were two scars—one on each side of Villas-Boas's chin. Fontes, who gave the young farmer a thorough physical examination, reported that he had found two "small hyperchromic spots, one on each side of the chin . . . scars resulting from some superficial lesion with associated bleeding under the skin."

The first mention of the Villas-Boas case in an American publication came in a 1962 review of Coral Lorenzen's book, *The Great Flying Saucer Hoax.* The book was a compendium of UFO sightings and evidence, and mentioned nothing about Villas-Boas himself. Max B. Miller, writing in *Fate,* suggested that Dr. Olavo Fontes might not be reliable because he had circulated a report of the "alleged rape of a Brazilian farmer by a somewhat uninhibited female from space."

Coral Lorenzen, understandably irritated by the reference, responded, "Dr. Fontes has earned a reputation for thoroughness, objectivity, and originality of thought. . . . The so-called rape case . . . was never published in the *APRO Bulletin* [a UFO

140

newsletter edited by Lorenzen], nor was it mentioned in my book for the simple reason that we do not feel that it was sufficiently authenticated."

Of course, in 1962 the Villas-Boas report was one of a kind. There had been contactees, but Villas-Boas didn't fit into that category. There had been occupant reports, and Lorenzen was one of the first to publish reports of alien beings. But in 1962 this case was too bizarre for anyone to accept as authentic.

The Hill Abduction:

Location: Highway 3 in the White Mountains of New Hampshire, north of Portsmouth.

Witnesses: Betty Hill
                Barney Hill

Encounter Type: Abduction

Craft Type: Cigar-shaped

Alien Type: Gray

Alien Characteristics: The beings were described as having a Mongoloid appearance, with broad, flat faces, large slanted eyes, and small, flattened noses—though Betty Hill originally said that "their noses were larger [longer] than the average size, although I have seen people with noses like theirs—like Jimmy Durante's." The leader had very large almond-shaped eyes that seemed to wrap around to the sides of his head. The mouth was a slit with a vertical line on either side. The skin had a bluish gray cast to it.

Home World: Zeta I, Zeta II Reticuli

Sources: *Interrupted Journey,* by John Fuller; *The October Scenario,* by Kevin D. Randle; *Flying Saucer Occupants,* by Coral Lorenzen; *High Strangeness: UFOs from 1960 Through 1979,* by Jerome Clark; *Encounters with UFO Occupants,* by Coral and Jim Lorenzen; *Watch the Skies!,* by Curtis Peebles; *Phenomenon,* by John Spencer and Hilary Evans; "Hypnosis and the Hill Abduction," by Mark Rodeghier, in the files of CUFOS/NICAP.

Reliability: 6

Narrative: On September 19, 1961, the Hills were returning from vacation, driving along a deserted section of Highway 3 in the White Mountains of New Hampshire. They had stopped for coffee about ten that night and believed they would arrive home before 3:00 A.M.

As they drove through the mountains, Betty Hill noticed a bright star near the moon. She was sure it hadn't been there before, and she was sure it was getting brighter. Finally she pointed it out to Barney, and he told her he thought it was an artificial satellite.

The bright star intrigued them. Several times during the next hour they stopped. Once or twice they got out a pair of binoculars to try to see any detail behind the light. Betty was now convinced they were looking at something out of the ordinary, but Barney kept insisting that it was nothing more unusual than an airplane, a satellite, or a very bright star.

During one of the stops, Barney used the binoculars to study the light. He saw red, amber, green, and blue lights rotating around it. To Barney it looked like an aircraft fuselage with no wings. He could hear no sound from engines. When he returned to the car, he was frightened. He didn't want Betty to know that, however, and he told her again that the object was just an airplane.

The object swooped down and began to pace the car. Betty watched through the binoculars and now could see a double row of windows. She demanded that Barney stop the car, but at first he refused. Finally he stopped in the middle of the road, and when Betty handed him the binoculars, he got out, leaving the engine running. Now he got a good look at the object, seeing for the first time that it was a large disc. Again he told Betty, "It must be a plane or something."

Although he was afraid, he stepped away from the car and walked across the road toward the object. He kept walking until he was about 50 feet from the craft, which was hovering just above the trees. Through the binoculars he could clearly see the double row of windows, and inside the ship he saw six beings. One, whom Barney thought of as "the leader," wore a black leather jacket.

As he watched, five of the six turned their backs and seemed to manipulate controls. The saucer began a slow descent. Fins holding red lights spread along the craft, and something, possibly landing gear, was lowered from the belly of the object.

Barney now focused on the remaining face and was overwhelmed by the feeling that he was going to be captured. He jerked the binoculars from his eyes, spun around, and ran back toward Betty and the car. Shouting that they were going to be kidnapped, he threw the binoculars on the backseat and slid behind the wheel. He slammed the car into gear and roared off as fast as possible. He ordered Betty to watch for the thing, but it had apparently disappeared.

As Barney began to calm down, they heard a series of strange electronic beeps. Both felt drowsy. The beeps came again just as they passed a sign that told them that Concord was 17 miles farther on. They continued home, arriving about five in the morning.

They unpacked before going to bed. Betty took a bath and, according to Coral Lorenzen, "for no reason whatsoever, bundled up the dress and shoes she had been wearing and shoved them into the deep recesses of her closet."

Six days after the event, Betty Hill wrote to Major Donald E. Keyhoe, a writer and director of the National Investigations Committee on Aerial Phenomena (NICAP), describing what had happened to her and her husband. She also suggested that she was thinking of finding a reputable psychiatrist to perform hypnotic regression to recover memories because Barney was having trouble remembering parts of the story.

Barney began to have stomach trouble. In December 1963, after consulting with two different doctors, he was sent on to Dr. Benjamin Simons, a well-known and highly qualified neurosurgeon who eventually used hypnosis on both the Hills.

Under hypnosis, Barney Hill told what happened after they heard the first beeps. For some reason Barney turned down a dirt road and drove up to a roadblock. There the engine quit, and several men appeared around the car. They guided the Hills through a wooded area to the craft, which was sitting on the ground.

Betty Hill later described the beings as having a Mongoloid appearance with broad, flat faces, large slanting eyes, and small, flattened noses. Barney added to the description, saying that the leader had very large, almond-shaped eyes that seemed to wrap around to the sides of his head. The mouth was a slit with a vertical line on either side. The skin, according to Betty, had a bluish gray cast to it.

According to the reports, Barney kept his eyes closed during most of the time they were on the craft. Some researchers have suggested that this is why his tale was never as rich in detail as that told by his wife. He did, however, mention an examination and that he was put on a table that was too short for him.

Betty described her examination, saying that unusual instruments touched her body in various places, that samples of skin and fingernails were taken, and that hair was pulled from her head. When a long needle was pushed into her navel, she screamed at the examiner, and the leader passed a hand over her eyes, stopping the pain.

Betty communicated with the leader, though there is no real indication that they spoke out loud. She had the impression that the leader was keeping the rest of the crew away from her. She was also told that she didn't have to worry about Barney, that he would be all right. During the discussion, she asked where the aliens had come from, and the leader showed her a map, allegedly of one portion of the galaxy, but asked Betty where the sun was. When Betty failed to identify it, he told her that the map would do her no good.

Betty was then escorted from the ship and joined Barney in the car. There was a second series of beeps, and when they "awakened," they were traveling down the road, nearing Concord.

The hypnotherapy by Dr. Benjamin Simons took several months. When it was over, Simons said that he thought the Hills were recounting a fantasy. He believed that Betty had originated the tale and shared it with Barney by telling him of her dreams. Simons believed this because Barney's account was less detailed than Betty's.

There is one other pertinent fact. The letter that Betty wrote to Major Keyhoe told much of the story in detail. Later, investigators reported that Barney sat in as Betty discussed the case with them. It is sometimes said that Barney and Betty didn't discuss the case between themselves, but Barney was always there when Betty was talking about the sighting. He certainly had plenty of opportunity to learn the details.

The star map that Betty saw while she was on the craft became one point of corroboration. Marjorie Fish, an Ohio teacher, spent years trying to find a pattern in the stars that matched the pattern drawn by Betty under hypnosis. She created a three-dimensional model of our section of the galaxy and then examined it from all angles, searching for a pattern. Her first attempts failed, but in 1972 after six years of intensive work, she finally discovered a pattern that matched what Betty Hill had drawn.

Fish discovered that the main stars in the map were Zeti I and Zeti II Reticuli, a star system about 37.5 light-years from Earth. The map showed what could be interpreted as lines of communication, with heavy lines between the closest stars and lighter lines between those farther away. A single line connected the sun into the mix, suggesting that the sun was a relatively unimportant star.

Walter Webb, at one time APRO's consultant in astronomy, wrote an analysis of Marjorie Fish's work. He was impressed by the fact that the lines on the map, as developed by Fish, connected stars that were exclusively the type defined as suited for supporting life on any planets that might be orbiting them. A random pattern of stars would not generate that sort of subtle, yet corroborative, evidence. Webb also wrote that "The pattern happens to contain a phenomenally high percentage of all the known stars suitable for life in our solar neighborhood."

Interestingly, according to Webb, Fish had believed that dozens of patterns would emerge. Instead, after six years of work, she found only a single pattern that met all the criteria. If the map was accurate and if Betty Hill had remembered the map correctly, then a good clue had been found about the location of one group of alien visitors. Of course, those were big ifs.

The Schirmer Abduction:

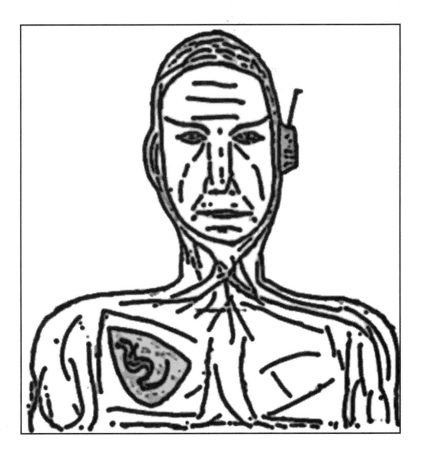

Location: Ashland, Nebraska

Witnesses: Herbert Schirmer

Encounter Type: Abduction

Craft Type: Disc

Alien Type: Humanoid

Alien Characteristics: The aliens were 4 1/2 to 5 feet tall. All wore close-fitting uniforms made of silver-gray material with boots and gloves. Each uniform had a hood like that of a pilot's helmet with a small antenna over the left ear. The skin on the visible parts of the face was gray-white, the nose flat, and the mouth merely a slit. The eyes were slanted with strange pupils that opened and closed like a camera lens.

Home World: Unknown

Sources: *Beyond Earth: Man's Contact with UFOs,* by Ralph and Judy Blum; *High Strangeness: UFOs from 1960 Through 1979,* by

150

Jerome Clark; *The October Scenario,* by Kevin D. Randle; *The Scientific Study of Unidentified Flying Objects,* edited by Daniel S. Gillmor.

Reliability: 5

Narrative: On December 3, 1967, Patrolman Herbert Schirmer was driving on the outskirts of Ashland, feeling that something was wrong. He saw a bull charging the gate of its corral, and Schirmer stopped to make sure the gate would hold. A couple of hours later he was near the intersection of Highway 63 when he saw something ahead of him. He thought it was a truck, but when he flipped on the high-beam headlights, the "truck" flashed up into the night sky.

When he returned to the police station early in the morning, he noted the flying saucer in his police report and thought nothing more about it. At home, he had a headache, a red welt on his neck, and a buzzing in his ears that kept him from sleeping.

Later his case came to the attention of the University of Colorado's air force–sponsored UFO investigation. Someone on the committee noticed that twenty minutes seemed to be missing from Schirmer's police log. It was suggested that hypnotic regression be used to see if the missing time could be accounted for.

Under hypnotic regression, Schirmer told of seeing a flying saucer. As it landed, he saw legs shoot from the bottom of it, telescoping from it. Although he wanted to get out of the area, he felt he was prevented from starting his police cruiser. Something in his mind made it impossible for him to get away.

As he sat there, a hatch or door opened, and the beings began to emerge. Schirmer tried to draw his weapon, but again he was prevented from doing so. The beings surrounded his car, and one of them pointed something at Schirmer. There was a bright flash, and he passed out momentarily. The next thing he remembered was rolling down the cruiser's window.

The aliens, according to him, were 4 1/2 to 5 feet tall. All wore close-fitting uniforms made of silver-gray material with boots and gloves. The uniforms all had a hood, like that of a pilot's helmet with a small antenna over the left ear. The visible skin of the face was gray-white, the nose flat, and the mouth merely a slit. The eyes were slanted with strange pupils that opened and closed like a camera lens.

Schirmer said that the beings communicated with him by voice and telepathy. The beings spoke broken English that sounded strange. The aliens told Schirmer that they had been studying human languages.

While Schirmer was on the ship, they provided him with some technical information. Their ships, according to him, are vulnerable to radar because of ionization. They have hidden bases on Earth, including one underwater near Florida and one in the polar region. According to Schirmer, they come from another galaxy not far from our galaxy. (It is assumed here that Schirmer meant to say "solar system," not "galaxy.") The leader showed Schirmer a "viewscreen" on which he saw three "warships" flying through space against a background of stars that included the Big Dipper.

The aliens told Schirmer that they had stolen electricity from power lines, but in amounts too small for power companies to detect. They also told him that they had been coming to Earth for a long time, observing human activity.

Before his release, the leader looked into Schirmer's eyes and said, "I wish you would not tell you have been aboard this ship." He told Schirmer precisely what to say about the incident: "You are to tell that the ship landed below in the intersection of the highways, that you approached and it shot up into the air. . . . We will return to see you two more times."

Investigation by the scientists of the Condon Committee resulted in some interesting conclusions. Schirmer was given a polygraph examination by an official agency. There were no indications of deception. Schirmer believed that he had seen a flying saucer. Psychological tests were also administered, with Schirmer's permission. Finally, Dr. Leo Sprinkle, a professor of psychology at the University of Wyoming, used hypnosis on Schirmer and discovered the "hidden memories." Sprinkle concluded that Schirmer believed in the reality of the events he described.

The final conclusion of the Condon Committee scientists was that "Evaluation of psychological assessment tests, the lack of any evidence, and interviews with the patrolman left project staff with no confidence that the trooper's reported UFO experience was physically real."

In defense of the Condon Committee scientists, it must be said that their conclusions were the only ones that could have been reached scientifically. No physical evidence was reported, and there was no corroboration of Schirmer's report. Clearly he believed he was telling the truth, but in a scientific inquiry additional evidence is needed. A report by a single eyewitness is not sufficient proof.

The Hickson-Parker Case:

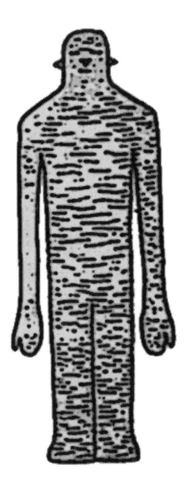

Location: Pascagoula, Mississippi

Witnesses: Charles Hickson (age 42)
　　　　　　Calvin Parker (19)

Encounter Type: Abduction

Alien Type: Robotic

Alien characteristics: The beings were about 5 feet tall and were covered with wrinkled gray skin. They had long arms that ended in lobsterlike claws, and their legs seemed to be fused together. The creatures made a buzzing sound.

Home World: Unknown

Sources: *The October Scenario,* by Kevin D. Randle; *The Encyclopedia of UFOs,* by Ronald Story; *High Strangeness: UFOs from 1960 Through 1979,* by Jerry Clark; *UFOs Explained,* by Philip Klass; *Watch the Skies,* by Curtis Peeples.

Reliability: 3

Narrative: This incident gained national attention during the 1973 wave. The two witnesses alerted a newspaper about what they had seen on October 12, 1973, in Pascagoula, Mississippi. According to Charles Hickson, then forty-two years old, he and a friend, Calvin Parker, then nineteen, were fishing from an old pier on the west bank of the Pascagoula River when a bright blue light attracted their attention. At first it was high overhead, but then it dropped toward the ground. Hickson later told investigators that it stopped only a few feet above the surface of the river. A buzzing noise was coming from it, but there was no wind or blast like that from a jet engine.

As he watched, one end of the object, an egg-shaped craft, opened, and three creatures floated from it. Hickson believed them to be about 5 feet tall. They were covered with wrinkled gray skin and had long arms that ended in lobsterlike claws. Their legs seemed to be fused together. The creatures, which seemed to be buzzing, headed for the men. The three beings separating so that one could pick up Parker, who had fainted, and the other two lifted Hickson and floated him toward the dimly glowing ship.

A door seemed to appear in the side of the craft, and they were floated through it. According to Hickson, he and Parker spent about twenty minutes on the ship. The interior was bare except for a device that Hickson thought looked like a big eye. Eventually he was floated back off the ship and deposited on the riverbank with Parker.

Hickson didn't see the UFO take off. He reported that he heard a buzzing sound and the UFO vanished. For a few minutes Hickson didn't know what to do. The story was so fantastic that he didn't think anyone would believe him. Besides, Parker, who was now conscious, was still terrified.

After several drinks in a local bar, Hickson decided that he should tell someone in authority. He walked to the newspaper office, but it was closed. Next he tried Kessler Air Force Base and received the now standard reply that the air force no longer investigated UFO sightings. The air force suggested that possibly the local sheriff or university would be interested.

Hickson opted for the sheriff, telling him that he had no desire for publicity, despite the fact he had visited a newspaper office first. Within hours, however, the story was national news and Hickson had more publicity than he dreamed possible.

The next morning Jim and Coral Lorenzen of the civilian Aerial Phenomena Research Organization (APRO) learned of the abduction and began making plans. All three of their psychology consultants were busy, but James A. Harder, their director of research, could travel to Pascagoula. Harder, a civil engineer, was versed in the use of hypnosis.

Dr. J. Allen Hynek had also heard the news reports and called APRO Headquarters to find out if they planned to investigate. Learning that Harder was being dispatched, Hynek made his own plans to fly to Pascagoula.

On Saturday morning the whole cast was assembled in the centrally located offices of the J. Walker Shipbuilders Company for the hypnosis session: Hickson, Parker, Hynek, Dr. Julius Bosco, Deputy Sheriff Barney Mathis, Police Detective Thomas Huntly, and Hickson's attorney, Joe Colingo.

Over two days the men examined the details of the abduction. Hickson confirmed much of his story, adding that the alien spaceship was 16 to 18 feet long and had a trapdoor in the back. He described the creatures for the assembled men.

Harder was impressed and told APRO Headquarters that it would have been nearly impossible for Hickson and Parker to have simulated their feelings of terror (an erroneous conclusion) while under hypnosis. Newsmen asked both Hynek and Harder for their opinions. Hynek suggested the men had a frightening experience but said that that didn't translate into an extraterrestrial event.

Reporters weren't as reserved in their opinions as Hynek and Harder, however. Headlines the next day screamed, "Scientists Believe UFO Story." That wasn't exactly right, but before the

157

claim could be corrected, reporters were off chasing another UFO event.

Late in the month, after Harder and Hynek had completed much of their investigation, a polygraph examination was arranged in New Orleans for Hickson. According to several sources, he passed the test, which took nearly two hours to complete. Newspapers claimed that the "lie test" proved the case.

Philip Klass, who launched his own investigation some days later, believed there was something wrong with the test. He wondered why it had been administered by an operator who had not yet finished his training, when qualified polygraph operators could have been found closer to Pascagoula. To Klass, this suggested the test had been rigged in Hickson's favor.

But Klass, Harder, and all the rest overlooked a couple of important points. The lie detector test would only suggest, to a reasonable certainty, that Hickson was telling the truth *as he believed it.* The test would not prove that Hickson and Parker were abducted, and it certainly would not suggest that the abduction had been at the hands of alien beings.

Two years later, in October 1975, Hickson attended a UFO conference held at Fort Smith, Arkansas. He had been invited to tell his story, on the condition that he submit to another lie detector test arranged by the conference organizers. Hickson agreed, but when the time came, he said his attorney had advised him not to take the test. Although many attorneys routinely advise their clients against taking such tests because they are so open to human interpretation, the controversy was stirred up again.

Other controversies surrounded the story. Hickson, for example, seemed to have no real idea precisely when he had seen the UFO, telling researchers and investigators at different times that it was about seven in the evening or maybe about eight or even as late as nine. Hickson told me that he never wore a watch because no matter how many he tried, they either ran fast or slow or stopped altogether. That does provide him with a good excuse for not knowing what time it was.

The controversy about the Hickson-Parker abduction continues to rage today. But what is important is not the 1973 wave of sightings or the final conclusions drawn based on those sightings but what the government reaction to them was. Although government officials claimed no interest and told all who called that they had completed their UFO investigations, evidence suggests that that isn't true.

The Roach Abduction:

Location: Lehi, Utah

Witnesses: Pat Roach
Bonnie Roach (age 13)
Debbie Roach (6)

Encounter Type: Abduction

Alien Type: Human and humanoid

Alien Characteristics: The alien creatures were described as small, with large heads, big eyes, and pasty white faces. The had long three-fingered hands. All wore shiny suits that looked like uniforms. Each being wore a kind of cap or helmet that hid the top of its head, and a Sam Browne belt with a chest strap that held a small pack. All of them wore gloves. The one female had long hair and wore a long skirt and a headband. The witnesses also reported a balding, graying human whom they thought of as a doctor.

Home World: Unknown

Sources: *The October Scenario,* by Kevin D. Randle; *Abducted,* by Coral Lorenzen; *The Encyclopedia of UFOs,* by Ronald Story.

Reliability: 2

Narrative: Pat Roach, a divorcée who lived with her children, reported that she and a number of her children were abducted from their house early on the morning of October 17, 1973. Just after midnight she was awakened, thinking that something strange had happened, but she didn't know what.

Although two of her daughters told her that "spacemen" had been in the house, Pat Roach refused to believe it. Instead, suspecting that there had been a prowler either in the house or in the yard, Roach called the police. They checked the area and the neighborhood but found nothing and saw nobody. Pat and her children were too upset to return to the house. They spent the night with friends.

For two years the family said little about the events. Unsure of what to do, Roach wrote to *Saga* magazine, asking for help. In the letter she mentioned the story of the spacemen, saying that she wanted to know what had happened.

Under hypnosis conducted by Dr. James A. Harder, a civil engineer in California, Pat Roach said that two smallish creatures were standing near her couch when she awakened. They reached down, touching her arms, and lifted her up. She saw some of her children in the room, struggling with other creatures. She then had the impression they were being lifted slightly and then floated outside to a waiting craft. Roach never really saw a ship; she just had the impression of a hatch at the top of a stairway.

Inside the craft she was separated from her children, taken to a room with a metal table that also seemed to float, and then given a gynecological examination. She was shown some of their technology, was hypnotized by the aliens and questioned about her past and her emotions, and was finally given her clothes and told to dress.

Her youngest child, Debbie, said that they all had been put on a machine run by an "Indian girl." According to Debbie, several of the neighbors were standing in a long line, waiting for their turn to "get on the machine."

The oldest girl, under hypnosis and questioning by Harder, remembered her mother being examined. Most important, she remembered seeing a human working with the alien creatures. She thought of him as a doctor and said that she knew he was human because he had a "regular ear."

Investigation of the case didn't reveal anything that would suggest that Roach had invented the tale. A review of the transcripts of the hypnotic sessions, however, shows that leading questions were asked repeatedly. That, in and of itself, makes some of the recovered information suspect.

The Aveley Abduction:

Location: Aveley, Essex, England

Witnesses: John Avis (age 32)
Elaine Avis (28)
Karen Avis (11)
Kevin Avis (10)
Stuart Avis (7)

Encounter Type: Abduction

Craft Type: Oval-shaped, blue light

Alien Type: Humanoid and hairy humanoid

Alien Characteristics: The humanoid was about 6 feet 8 inches tall. It was completely covered by a seamless one-piece rubber suit. The eyes, which were visible, were larger than human and pink. The hands had three digits, and the skin was very pale and nearly translucent.

The hairy humanoids were only about 4 feet tall. Each one had bushy brown hair all over its face and hands, two large triangular eyes, a light brown beak for a nose, and a slit for a mouth. Their large, hairy hands had four digits with claws on them. They were wearing large, loose-fitting white gowns.

Home World: Unknown

Sources: "The Aveley Abduction," by Andrew Collins in *Flying Saucer Review*, April 1978.

Reliability: 6

Narrative: The family, while driving home from a visit to Elaine's parents, noticed a bright blue oval light that seemed to be pacing them. Although they originally thought it might be a helicopter, they decided after several minutes that it was a UFO.

They drove on, passed a public house that was well lighted, and continued onto a road where there was little or no traffic. The road dipped and turned, and just after they had gone around one bend, they spotted a green fog or mist obscuring the road. As they approached it, the radio began to crackle and smoke, and the headlights dimmed as the engine quit. They rolled into the fog, which they later described as cold. They heard no sounds from anywhere, but each reported a tingling sensation.

Their next conscious memory was of being beyond the fog and driving toward home. Once they reached home, still somewhat frightened by the ordeal, Elaine noticed that they had arrived nearly an hour and a half later than they should have. That concerned them greatly, but they were not sure what it meant.

Although both John and Elaine thought they had better just forget about the experience, they contacted a large local UFO group after reading about it in the newspaper. They apparently hoped that the UFO investigators would be able to answer some of their questions about the ordeal.

After a series of meetings with UFO researchers, hypnotic regression sessions were arranged. Under the influence of hypnosis, John revealed that after entering the green mist, there was a shaft or column of light. The car, including the occupants, was lifted by the light and came to rest inside what appeared to be a large hangar. John remembered standing on a balcony, looking down at a car, which he believed was his. He could not explain how he had gotten from the car to the balcony.

Standing next to him was his wife and maybe his older son. Behind them on the balcony was a tall creature. John and the tall creature moved off to the left, and he suddenly had the sensation of rising again. He found himself inside a room with a table in it. The tall creature touched John on the shoulder, and he lost consciousness.

When he came to, he was lying on the table. Some kind of device was moving from his head down toward his feet. As the device moved along his body, he felt warm pressure on his skin. The device seemed to be under the control of small, ugly, hairy creatures, who he noticed were in the room around him.

When the examination was over, John swung his legs off the table and sat up. He asked many questions, all of which were answered. When he asked for a tour of the ship, the request was granted. During the tour, he saw a number of star maps, which he described as circles with lines connecting them. Apparently similar to the one that Betty Hill had seen. Eventually he was taken into a darkened room and shown holograms of the aliens' home world as it looked after it was ruined by pollution and natural disasters.

After the planetarium-style show, the leader told John it was time for him to return. He said that they would meet again, and the next thing John knew, he was back inside the car.

Under hypnosis, Elaine told a similar tale about the car stalling in the green mist and then ascending in a pillar of light. Her next memory was of standing on the balcony with her husband. Then, after being led away, she descended through a hole that appeared in the wall.

She saw a table surrounded by instruments. She was led to the table and strapped on it. When she began to struggle, one of the tall creatures pushed through the small hairy ones and told her to relax. He said they couldn't do anything with her if she struggled. Then he touched her head, and she lost consciousness.

The next thing she remembered was walking along a corridor. Then she was inside a control room, where she conversed with another of the tall creatures. She was shown a table with food, which she was about to refuse to sample when it was taken away.

She was shown different things, and she listened to music that relaxed her. She was also shown a series of holograms that seem to match, generally, those shown to her husband. She was told to touch the ball in the room, which she did. The leader told her that it was time for her to leave but that they would meet again.

Unlike her husband, who woke up in the car, she remembered getting dressed and telling her husband to hurry and to give Kevin a hand. She also recalled drinking something quickly. Then everything faded, and she was suddenly standing on a catwalk around the car.

Elaine told the aliens that she didn't want to leave, but she was told that she had to. Again she lost consciousness. She awoke in the car. She felt a jolt and the experience was over.

The Diaz Abduction:

JANUARY 4, 1975

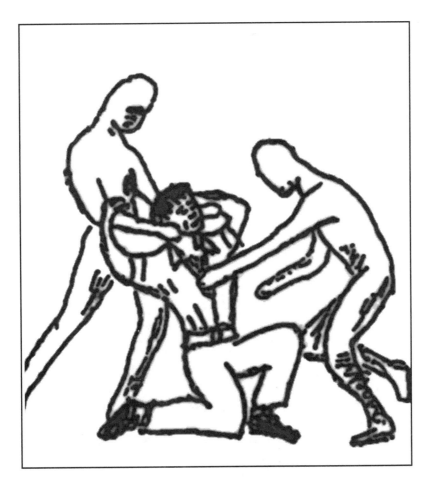

Location: Bahía Blanca, Argentina

Witnesses: Carlos Diaz (age 28)

Encounter Type: Abduction

Craft Type: Unknown

Alien Type: Humanoid

Alien Characteristics: The beings stood about 5 feet tall and had a greenish tint to their skin, which felt like sponge rubber. Their faces were smooth with no mouth, nose, or ears, and they had no hair at all. They also had no hands; their arms seemed to end in stumps that had suckers at the ends. They wore no clothing.

Home World: Unknown

Sources: *High Strangeness: UFOs from 1960 Through 1979*, by Jerome Clark; *Encounters with UFO Occupants*, by Coral and Jim Lorenzen; *The Diaz Abduction in Argentina*, by Joseph Brill in *Official UFO*, February 1976.

Reliability: 0

Narrative: Diaz, returning home after work, had just exited a bus when a powerful beam of light came from the sky. Although his house was only about 100 yards away, he couldn't move. He said that he heard a quiet buzzing around him. He felt a current of air that lifted him up about 8 feet, and he lost consciousness.

When he awoke, he was inside a sphere. He wanted to get up but couldn't make his arms and legs work. The floor of the sphere was made of hard plastic, and the walls were made of some translucent material. Small holes in the sphere allowed air to enter. Diaz said that he felt ill if he turned away from those small holes. He was alone in the sphere, which he thought was 9 or 10 feet in diameter. It seemed to be moving at a high rate of speed.

Diaz thought he had been inside the sphere for fifteen minutes when three beings approached him from behind. Two of them tried to subdue him. They seemed to be trying to pull hair from his head. One of them would hold him, and the other would take hold of his hair. Although the creatures moved slowly, they were very strong, according to Diaz. As the struggle continued, he began to feel dizzy, and he passed out once again.

He was awakened by a man some time later and taken to a hospital. Although he still had the newspaper that he had bought earlier, he learned that he was in Buenos Aires, more than 200 miles from his home.

Diaz was reportedly examined by about fifty different doctors and interviewed by local military authorities. The newspaper that he had purchased near his home, according to some researchers, was additional corroboration for his tale. There didn't seem to be any way for him to have gotten from his home to Buenos Aires in the time allotted for it.

Jerome Clark, however, noted that Roberto Enrique Banchs, a noted ufologist in South America, had investigated the case and found "numerous discrepancies" that suggested the sighting could not have progressed as Diaz had claimed.

More Tujunga Canyon Events:

Location: Panorama City, California

Witnesses: Lori Briggs
Jo Maine

Encounter Type: Abduction

Craft Type: Dome-shaped object

Alien type: Humanoid

Alien Characteristics: These beings had large heads and big eyes. They were so extremely thin that it seemed impossible that the bodies could hold up the large heads. Each alien's face was elongated like an egg, and there was a small nose and a small mouth. The beings seemed to be bald. Bright lights seemed to shine from the eyes.

Home World: Unknown

Sources: *The Tujunga Canyon Contacts*, by Ann Druffel and D. Scott Rogo.

Reliability: 1

Narrative: The witness was sound asleep in her apartment when she suddenly awoke and found herself paralyzed. She realized that there were beings or people in the room with her. She saw hands that were very thin and very long, and she believed that the creatures were short. She was lying on her back and felt that she was looking right into the eyes of the creature. She didn't know how long the experience lasted.

That was in 1970. Five years later Lori Briggs was again awakened in the middle of the night under similar circumstances. Voices inside her head told her to go with the creatures she believed were in the room with her.

With those tales in mind, researchers induced Briggs to undergo hypnotic regression in an attempt to learn if there was more to the strange nocturnal visitations. The reports by Briggs suggested all the symptoms of the classic abduction.

Under hypnosis, she recalled waking with the beings standing right next to her. They wanted her to go with them. She didn't want to go, but somehow her will was bent to theirs, and the next thing she knew, she was going with them. The creatures floated above the ground and took her through the apartment walls. In a matter of seconds she was inside the alien craft.

Inside the craft she saw a table that looked and felt as if it was made of pink stone, but it sometimes turned transparent. There was a bright light source beneath the table. She believed that it was some kind of X-ray device and that they shined different kinds of light through it. She was placed on the table and examined by the alien creatures.

Briggs was unsure about what happened next. Either they returned her to her apartment or she decided it was time to go and pushed a button to open the door. The aliens told her to wait, saying that they would go with her.

Back in the apartment, her roommate was still asleep, undisturbed by the activity around her. Back in the bed, Briggs found herself paralyzed again. She remembered almost nothing of the experience when she woke up the next morning, only the terror of waking in the middle of the night and being unable to move as something stared at her.

Jo Maine, her roommate, was also interviewed and hypnotized. Though her memories of the events were not as complete as those of her roommate, she did recall the events of that night in July. She mentioned, independently, that she had seen the bright lights and that she felt as if she was floating. She found herself in a tubelike area with light all around her. She didn't know how she had gotten out of the apartment and into the tube.

She remembered lying flat in the dark. After some sort of an examination she was covered and forced to another location. Then she was suddenly back in the apartment with Lori lying next to her in bed.

The Walton Experience:

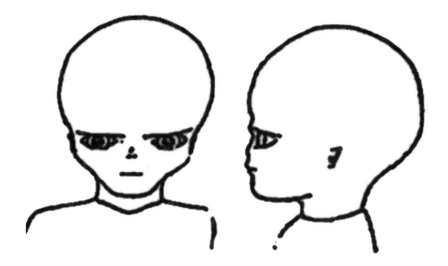

Location: Snowflake, Arizona

Witnesses: Travis Walton
Mike Rogers
Allen Dalis
John Goulette
Dwayne Smith
Kenneth Peterson
Steve Pierce

Encounter Type: Abduction

Alien Type: Gray, human

Alien Characteristics: The aliens were small creatures, about 5 feet tall, dressed in loose-fitting orange jumpsuits. According to Walton, they had high, domed heads, large eyes, and tiny noses, mouths, and ears. They were dressed in coveralls. Their hands had five fingers and fingernails. To Walton, the creatures looked frail, with soft, marshmallowlike skin.

Walton also described a man dressed in blue coveralls. To Walton, he appeared to be a normal-looking human being wearing a transparent bubblelike helmet. The man was about 6 feet 2, weighed about 200 pounds, and had long hair that covered his ears.

Home World: Unknown

Sources: *The October Scenario,* by Kevin Randle; *The Encyclopedia of UFOs,* by Ronald Story; *Abducted,* by Coral and Jim Lorenzen; *High Strangeness: UFOs from 1960 Through 1979,* by Jerome Clark; *UFO Abductions,* by Philip Klass; *Watch the Skies,* by Curtis Peeples.

Reliability: 2   The low rating is due to the failed lie detector tests, as well as the evolving nature of the tale.

Narrative: According to the original report and Travis Walton himself, the witnesses had been cutting trees on a Forest Service contract in Apache-Sitgreaves National Forest in November 1975. Walton, along with crew leader Mike Rogers, and fellow workers Allen Dalis, John Goulette, Dwayne Smith, Kenneth Peterson, and Steve Pierce, had worked all day thinning the undergrowth and stacking the material in accordance with the governmental regulations under which they worked. After the long day, all looked forward to getting home, cleaning up, and relaxing. There was even talk of swimming at an indoor pool in Snowflake, Arizona.

The men had climbed into their car and headed toward home when Walton, or possibly Allen Dalis, thought he saw a glow through the trees. Others then saw the light too and urged the driver, Rogers, to head toward it. They drove through the trees along a road that was little more than a track, came out of a stand of pines, and had an unobstructed view of the alien craft hovering over a clearing in front of them. They now knew they were looking at a flying saucer and not the setting sun, the headlights of another car, or a large campfire.

They later described the craft as a luminous disc hovering 15 to

20 feet above a pile of cut trees, branches, and scrub brush. The craft, which was about 100 feet from the truck, measured about 20 feet in diameter and was maybe 8 feet thick. Dark silver vertical lines, longer than they were wide, divided its surface into panel-like geometrical forms. A thin band with a protruding ridge circled the middle of the craft. The ship's milky yellow glow illuminated the ground around it and the trees surrounding the clearing.

Rogers shut off the truck's engine, and as Walton opened the door, someone said quietly, "That's a UFO." Years later Walton would write, "I was afraid it would fly away and I would miss the chance of a lifetime to satisfy my curiosity about it. I hurriedly got out of the truck and started toward the hovering ship."

Walton walked forward. He could hear a whine of machinery from inside the vessel. The golden glow of the disc bathed him in light. Then, Walton wrote, "I was startled by a powerful, thunderous swell in the volume of the vibrations from the craft. . . . I saw the saucer start wobbling on its axis with a quickening motion. . . . I ducked into a crouch, down behind the safety of a nearby log."

Walton didn't see what happened next. He had decided it was time to get away, but as he rose from his crouch, a beam reached out. He felt a paralyzing blow as he was thrown backward. In his latest book, he wrote, "I saw and heard nothing. All I felt was a numbing force of a blow that felt like a high-voltage electrocution." He hit the ground and was still.

He would later learn that he was lifted off the ground, his body arched backward, his arms and legs outstretched. He flew back about 10 feet and hit the rocky ground on his right shoulder. He sprawled on the ground, limp and motionless.

His friends in the truck, sure that he had been killed by the flying saucer and the beam of blue light, screamed at Rogers. He started the engine, backed up, turned, and raced toward the track that led from the area. The bouncing of the truck on the rough, nearly invisible road forced Rogers to slow down. He swerved to miss a tree and finally stopped.

Standing outside the truck, the men discussed what to do next. One or two thought Walton was dead, but others thought they should return to look for him. As they climbed back into the truck, Rogers caught a glimpse of something streaking away. He thought it might be the golden ship and was impressed by its rate of acceleration. He was the only one who reported seeing the streak of light.

The men searched the area but failed to find any sign of Travis Walton. They argued about the location where they had seen the ship. They argued about the location where they had last seen Walton. They argued about what to do next. They were so badly frightened by the events and by the disappearance of Walton that even the moon now surprised and scared them. Finally they decided to alert the local authorities.

They telephoned the sheriff and told Deputy Chuck Ellison, who responded, that Travis Walton was missing and might be dead. The deputy called for help, and a search was organized later that night. It continued the following day, but no trace of Walton was found. Duane Walton, the missing man's brother, said that when he drove into the area the next morning, he saw no sign of a search party. He demanded an explanation, and by noon, searchers were again out looking for his brother.

One day during the search, a man in a Forest Service uniform appeared with a Geiger counter. According to Travis Walton's latest book, the stranger tested the ground around the supposed abduction site but never got close to the actual spot where the events occurred. When he checked the hard hats worn by Walton's fellow workers, however, he found signs of radioactivity. This is an interesting aberration but it's of little real importance, especially since no one seems to know who the man was or what he was doing there.

While Walton was missing, the other members of the work crew were given a lie detector test. The examiner, Cy Gilson, suggested that the men were telling the truth about the disappearance of Walton. It seems that the sheriff had suspected that they had murdered Walton and concocted the flying saucer story as a cover. The polygraph suggested that Rogers and his crew had not killed Walton. It didn't mean that Walton had been abducted or even that there was a UFO event. The purpose of the test had been to determine if Walton had been killed by accident or murdered by the crew.

According to Walton and others, all of the men passed this examination except Dalis. Later, in his book, Walton wrote, "After little more than an hour, Allen stormed out of the testing room. He loudly cursed the examiner and slammed the door behind him."

The test results showed that the men were telling the truth. Cy Gilson, the polygrapher, in an unofficial report given to Mike Rogers and the others at the completion of the sessions, said, according to the reconstructed dialogue, "When I started testing you men this morning, I really expected to find that a murder had been committed. After all those hard words this morning, and the way Allen Davis [sic] reacted, I was even more sure of foul play. But none of the tests except Allen's showed anything like that."

In the official police report, Case Number 23-75-56, Sheriff's Deputy Ellison wrote, "On Monday, November 10, the six men who were with Walton at the time of his disappearance were subjected to polygraph tests at their own request, and of the six all of them passed the test with a positive reading. The fifth man [Allen Dalis] was inconclusive on one phase of the test but it was stated that he 'had basically told the truth.'"

During all this, the searches continued but failed to find a trace of Walton or his body. All were perplexed until Walton reappeared five days later, dirty, tired, and slightly confused. He awoke feeling cold, according to him, along a stretch of highway. Hovering over the highway was a silver disc that suddenly streaked into the sky, disappearing. Walton stood up, looked at the highway, and recognized it. He stumbled down the road, found a phone at a gas station, and tried to call his sister for help. He spoke to Grant Neff, his brother-in-law, who at first believed it was another of the many crank calls that had plagued the family after Walton's disappearance was reported by the media. The voice on the phone did not sound like Travis.

Neff, finally convinced that the voice belonged to Walton, drove to Snowflake, Arizona, to find Travis's brother, Duane, at the home of his mother, Mary Walton Kellett. Neff told them about the telephone call and said he was on his way to Heber.

In Heber, the two men found Walton crouched in a phone booth at the Exxon service station, shivering in the cold. He was conscious but seemed dazed and confused.

After Neff and Duane picked him up, Walton said little about what had happened, but he told them about the big eyes of the creatures he had encountered. His comments were vague and sightly incoherent. "They kept looking at me," he said repeatedly. The men didn't immediately understand what Walton was trying to tell them.

Although he'd been gone for five days, Walton seemed to think that only a couple of hours had passed. When told he had been missing for five days, he was stunned. At his sister's home, he talked briefly to friends and family about the ordeal, preferring to say as little as possible. He cleaned up in the bathroom and, for some reason, stepped on a scale. He had lost about 10 pounds during the five days he had been missing. This fact would become important later. Almost everyone who writes about the Walton case mentions those lost pounds.

According to all of the accounts, Walton remembered little about those missing five days, other than seeing the UFO and being struck by the beam of light. His first memory, after being hit by the beam, was of awakening in what he thought was a hospital room. The air seemed wet and heavy, and he had difficulty breathing. The details of his surroundings didn't register right away. Slowly he became aware that three small creatures, about 5 feet tall and dressed in loose-fitting orange jumpsuits, were standing around him.

Walton climbed to his feet and shouted at the creatures. He

pushed one of them into another. They seemed to him to be light-weight. He grabbed a cylindrical tube from a shelf and, believing it to be glass, tried to shatter it to make a weapon. It wouldn't break, but Walton swung it around. The beings keep their distance and finally turned and left the room through a door behind them.

He walked to the door, which he said was of "normal" height and was rectangular with rounded corners. He ran from the room and hurried down a corridor until he came to another room on his right. Looking in, he saw that it was round, and he could see the stars through the ceiling. It isn't clear if he was looking outside the craft or seeing star fields on some kind of equipment. The effect seemed to be of sitting in a chair in the middle of space. Maybe a better analogy would be of sitting in a planetarium as the night sky is projected onto the dome.

In the center of the room was a high-backed metallic chair. Walton wasn't sure if anyone was sitting in it because the back was to him. Cautiously he entered the room and found the chair unoccupied. He sat down and found a lever on the left arm of the chair. When he moved it, the stars seemed to move. When he let go, the lever returned to its original position. The stars stopped rotating and seemed to freeze in the new positions. He manipulated the lever again, but let go, fearing that he would do some real damage to the craft or the equipment. On the other arm were buttons, but Walton didn't experiment with them.

He got out of the chair and examined the wall. The lights came on and the stars faded. He walked back to the chair and heard some noise. Looking toward the doorway, he saw a man in blue coveralls standing there. To Walton he appeared to be a normal-looking human being wearing a transparent bubblelike helmet. This is one of the first references by an abductee to human beings working with an alien crew.

Walton tried to ask questions, but the man only smiled back at him. Walton later described the man as about 6 feet 2, weighing about 200 pounds and having long hair that covered his ears.

The man motioned to Walton and took him by the arm. Together they walked through the ship and out onto what seemed to be a hangar deck. He looked back at the craft and thought that it resembled the one he had seen in the forest, only much larger. The hangar deck held three or four similar craft.

He and his escort crossed the hangar deck and entered another small room, where Walton saw two men and a woman, dressed like his guide. Since they weren't wearing helmets, Walton thought they might hear his questions, but they merely looked at him. Then the guide crossed the room and exited, leaving Walton with the three beings.

It was at this point that Walton was apparently examined by the aliens. They took his arms and guided him to a nearby table. They gestured for him to climb up on the table, but he refused, struggling with them. They forced him to lie on the table on his back, and they put an oxygen mask–like device over his mouth and nose. He wanted to tear it from his face, but before he could act, he lost consciousness again.

That was all he remembered about the missing five days. His next conscious thought occurred when he awoke along the roadside with the ship hovering nearby. He could see the road and his surroundings reflected in its shiny metallic surface. His first real thought was to get some help or to call his family. That was when he walked down the road and, reaching the service station, made the phone call to his brother-in-law.

With his reappearance, a controversy erupted. Within days he was given a lie detector test, which he failed. A second test, given within six months is another point of controversy. Although the operator said Walton passed, the man's boss, after examining the records, suggested that Walton had not passed. A third test, given twenty years later, is probably invalid because of the length of time that had passed since the events. Although a great deal has been written about the Walton abduction, the important point is that Walton flunked his first test, probably flunked the second, and has never provided any solid evidence that the abduction was real. This explains the low reliability rating.

Another Multiple Abduction:

JANUARY 6, 1976

Location: Liberty, Kentucky

Witnesses: Mary Louise Smith
Mona Stafford (age 36)
Elaine Thomas

Encounter Type: Abduction

Craft Type: Disc with round windows

Alien Type: Gray, humanoid

Alien Characteristics: These small gray-skinned creatures had large, dark, slanted eyes with pupils. No other facial features were reported, and they were not described from the waist down. They were dressed in surgical gowns and masks.

Home World: Unknown

Sources: *High Strangeness: UFOs from 1960 Through 1979,* by Jerome Clark; *Encounters with UFO Occupants,* by Coral and Jim Lorenzen.

Reliability: 2

Narrative: Returning home by car after a birthday celebration, the witnesses saw an intense red glow in the eastern sky. The glow grew, coming closer, until it was hovering at treetop level near the car. All three women saw the domed disc, which flashed three shafts of bluish white light on the highway.

Smith, the driver, stopped the car and got out. Stafford pulled her back. Everything around them was dead silent. Smith, with tears streaming down her face, felt the onset of a terrific headache. The others were in the same state.

The lights on the craft went out, and Smith realized they were racing down the road. Smith couldn't slow the car down and asked her friends for help. She felt the car was being "pulled" down the highway. A moment later the terrain around them began to look familiar. She saw that they were getting close to their homes. When they reached the house, they realized that there was a period of missing time.

One of the UFO researchers who investigated the case was the late Len Stringfield. During his interview, he showed the women a number of drawings of aliens reported by others. Stafford pointed to one of them, saying it was what she had seen.

Although there had been a number of interviews, no funds were available for any additional work. The researchers needed, or rather wanted, to bring in someone to use hypnosis to gather additional data. Jerry Black, a researcher living in Indiana, negotiated a deal with the *National Enquirer* to bring in Dr. Leo Sprinkle.

Although all three women underwent hypnosis, no clear, coherent story of the abduction was obtained. Stafford, for example, remembered being taken from the car and later found herself lying in a hot, dark room. A white light seemed to force her back as an "eyelike" device examined her. Several small creatures surrounded her, all wearing surgical masks and gowns.

Thomas remembered either leaving the car or being taken from it and then being in a chamber with a window. She described humanoid creatures about 4 feet tall with dark eyes set in gray skin. She described a "cocoon" around her neck that choked her when she tried to speak. A bullet-shaped object was placed above her left breast.

Smith didn't remember an abduction, as such, but did remember the car being pulled backward. She was then surrounded by darkness with intense heat that burned her. She had the impression that she was being examined. She refused to undergo a second hypnosis session during that weekend session with Sprinkle.

Over time more memories were "recovered." Stafford said she knew that the creatures had separated her from her friends and that she was taken from one ship to another. She also said she believed she was in a cave or inside a volcano.

Stafford later reported that she'd had another encounter with an alien creature. She refused to obey the "telepathic" commands of a being in a gold robe. She believed that she was under the control of the alien creatures.

Stafford wasn't the only one to report a second encounter. Smith awoke one night and felt compelled to drive to the encounter site. She stood there for a while, unable to leave. She finally ran to her car at about three o'clock in the morning. She noticed that three of her rings were missing. They couldn't have come off by accident, and she did remember a tugging at her hands while she stood in the field.

Thomas, who died in 1978, was unnerved by the encounter and frequently called Sprinkle for information and advice. All three of the women told Sprinkle of paranormal experiences that they associated with their UFO experience.

The Allagash Abductions:

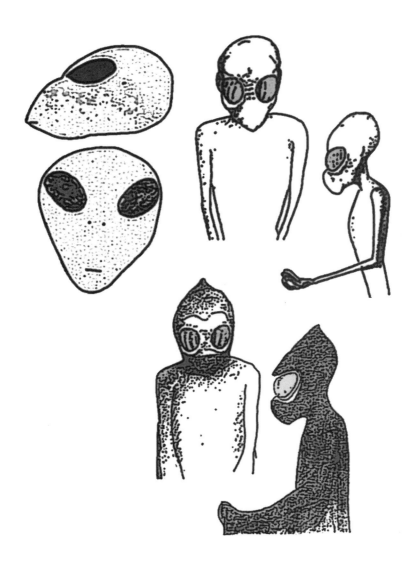

Location: Allagash Wilderness Waterway, Maine

Witnesses: Charlie Foltz
Chuck Rak
Jack Weiner
Jim Weiner

Encounter Type: Abduction

Craft Type: Saturn-shaped

Alien Type: Gray

Alien Characteristics: The beings were shorter than humans, with large heads, pointed chins, and large dark eyes. Their heads were out of proportion to the bodies, which were thin. Their arms and legs were very thin, and the hands had four fingers that were semiopposed.

Home World: Unknown

Sources: *The Allagash Abductions,* by Raymond E. Fowler.

Reliability: 4

Narrative: Raymond Fowler, author of *The Watchers*, in which he describes his own abduction, met Jim Weiner prior to speaking at a PSI symposium sponsored by the Universalist-Unitarian church in May 1988. Weiner had attended the conference on the advice of his doctor in the hope of finding someone who was knowledgeable about UFO abductions.

According to Fowler in *The Allagash Abductions*, Weiner had been plagued by nightmares for a number of years. The dreams centered around strange creatures looking at him, temporary paralysis, and a manipulation of the area around his genitals. Weiner told Fowler that he'd seen a UFO close at hand and that his brother and friends, who had also witnessed the sighting, had been having similar nightmares.

The sighting itself was interesting. The men, who were in a canoe, reported watching a point of light grow as if coming toward them. The object stopped above them and played a searchlight on the water around them. They watched the object for a while, then decided to return to shore. When they got to the shore, their fire had burned down and they wondered just how long they had been on the water.

Importantly, Weiner told Fowler that he had read Whitley Streiber's *Communion* and believed that Streiber's experiences mirrored his own. He also mentioned a period of missing time, the additional witnesses to the abduction, and the nightmares about the alien creatures. This information intrigued Fowler, especially the suggestion of a multiple-witness aspect to the abduction.

After meeting with Weiner, Fowler decided that the case demanded an investigation. He arranged for Weiner to undergo hypnotic regression in a number of sessions. While under hypnosis, Weiner described the first sighting of the UFO, which Fowler suggests might have been Jupiter. Then, two nights later, the object was back, coming closer to the four men in their canoe. Under hypnosis, Weiner remembered that it had hovered above them, played a light across them and the boat, and then disappeared. Weiner told Fowler they had built a large fire on the shore to serve as a beacon, but when they returned to the beach after the UFO disappeared, the fire had burned down to glowing coals, suggesting to Weiner that an hour had passed that was unaccounted for. It suggested they had been on the water much longer than Weiner had thought. It was the classic missing-time scenario.

During that first hypnosis session, Weiner merely related the story of the sighting. He expressed his surprise that the fire had burned down so fast. Fowler asked, "If there is time unaccounted for, why can't you remember?"

Weiner replied, "I don't know. I—I'd swear I remembered everything that happened."

At that point Fowler and the hypnotherapist, Tony Constantino, put Weiner into a deeper state of hypnosis and began probing again. Constantino then said, "You sense there is something you should remember?"

As the questioning continued, Weiner finally described events on board the craft but refused to describe the faces of the alien beings. It was clear to the men conducting the research that Weiner was suppressing much information.

At the conclusion of the first session, Fowler was "struck by the emotions that Jim manifested when reliving the experience." He also wondered if "the aliens programmed them not to see their faces or whether the sight of them caused self-imposed amnesia."

Fowler also told Weiner that they would talk more about UFO abductions once the investigation was over. Fowler advised him to refrain from talking to his fellow abductees so as not to taint the investigation. After eight years of discussion among the four men and the fact that Weiner had already read Streiber's work, however, contamination had already taken place.

After the second session in which Jim Weiner described the faces of the creatures for the first time, Fowler wrote, "I remembered Jim telling me about a series of lifelike nightmares involving bedroom visitations by alien creatures and paranormal happenings."

At the end of that session Fowler asked Jim Weiner, "When did you see the creatures again?"

"In Texas."

"What year was that?"

"I think it was 1980."

Fowler continued the investigation, talking to all of the men involved. Each remembered the UFO sightings, and each seemed to recall the period of missing time. Under close questioning by Fowler, each man described an abduction. Each drew the creatures that he had seen on the craft.

Fowler discovered that the UFO had stopped to hover over them. A beam of light, not unlike a searchlight, played across the lake. The men, in a panic, rowed frantically for the shore. The next thing they remembered was standing there watching the object disappear.

The hypnosis revealed that they were taken from the canoe to the object. Once inside the craft, they were stripped. Three sat on a bench while the fourth underwent a series of medical procedures. Skin scrapings were taken, blood was drawn, and semen was gathered.

The men said that the interior of the craft was cold. One of them said it reminded him of a doctor's office—sterile and cold. They all talked of a probing of their bodies and the use of what looked like a doctor's instruments.

None of the men wanted to remember the faces of the creatures. At first, the drawings and descriptions lacked that detail. But finally, under continued questioning, they all provided descriptions of the alien beings and the procedures they followed.

Once the examinations were completed, the men were dressed and returned to their camp. They watched the object disappear. Then, instead of discussing the strange event, they all felt extremely tired, so they turned in for the night.

The next morning, as they prepared to complete their trip, they didn't talk about the events of the night before. It was almost as if it had never happened.

Many believe that this case, because there were multiple witnesses, adds a level of credibility to the abduction phenomenon. The men couldn't have been suffering from a common delusion. There is no natural explanation for the fact that all of the men told virtually the same story while under hypnosis. For many, this case proves that abductions are real.

A Three-Eyed Creature:

DECEMBER 6, 1978

Location: Marzano, Genoa, Italy

Witnesses: Fortunato Zanfretta (age 26)

Encounter Type: Abduction

Craft Type: Triangular

Alien Type: Humanoid

Alien Characteristics: This alien was a 10-foot-tall being covered with thick greenish hair. It had two very large triangular eyes that inclined upward. In the folds of the skin above those eyes, there seemed to be a third, more human-shaped eye. There were pointed ears on the sides of the head.

Home World: Unknown

Sources: "Italian Night-Watchman Kidnapped by UFO," in *Flying Saucer Review.*

Reliability: 4

Narrative: Fortunato Zanfretta, a security guard or night watch-man, thought he saw four lights moving inside the courtyard of an unoccupied house. He tried to call his office to report the disturbance, but his car lights and his two-way radio failed. He then walked to the front gate of the courtyard as the lights first moved toward him and then disappeared behind the house.

Zanfretta worked his way to the corner of the house, but when he tried to look around it, he was pushed to the ground. He turned slightly and saw a creature, which suddenly vanished. As he scrambled to his feet and fled to his car, he heard a loud whistling sound behind him, and he felt a wave of heat.

As he called for help on the radio, which now worked, he noticed that it was after midnight, later than he thought it should be. He then fainted near his car, and an hour later his friends found him in a field. They also discovered a horseshoe-shaped depression about 24 feet wide.

A couple of weeks later, under hypnotic regression, Zanfretta described his abduction at the hands of the tall, hairy creatures. He was taken into a large round room, where the creatures put something on his head that caused him a great deal of pain.

The Intruders Case:

JUNE 30, 1983

Location: Copley Woods, Indiana

Witnesses: Debbie Jordan (reported as Kathy Davis)

Encounter Type: Abduction

Craft Type: Balls of light

Alien Type: Gray

Alien Characteristics: The alien was a classic gray, including the inverted teardrop-shaped head, large black eyes, holes for the nose, and a slit for the mouth.

Home World: Unknown

Sources: *Intruders,* by Budd Hopkins; *World Atlas of UFOs,* by John Spencer; *Abducted,* by Debbie Jordan and Kathy Mitchell.

Reliability: 5

Narrative: After seeing lights in her garden, Debbie Jordan went outside to see them better. Outside the house she attracted the attention of those in the craft and was taken aboard for medical experimentation. During this abduction, a small device was implanted in her body. She awakened in the garden in her nightgown, bleeding from the medical procedures performed. During this abduction she believes she met a child who was the result of her earlier abductions.

The June 30 abduction, which drew the attention of researchers, was obviously not the first that she experienced. During repeated hypnotic regression sessions, she told of abductions from her early childhood. She told of her mother protecting her from an airborne threat by forcing her to hide in the closet. The implication is that her mother had been abducted before her and was attempting to protect her from being taken.

On another occasion, in what UFO investigator Budd Hopkins thinks of as a screened memory, Jordan remembered meeting a little boy on a spacecraft. Hopkins believes this was actually an alien and that the idea of a little boy was implanted to disguise the abduction.

Jordan also reported under hypnosis that in December 1977 she was abducted from a car. The other occupants were "switched off," she said, so that they had no knowledge of the abduction and couldn't corroborate it. This was the first time she was given a gynecological examination by her abductors. According to Hopkins, she was also impregnated by the aliens at this time. Before the birth of the child, however, she was abducted again, and the fetus was removed.

In November 1983 she reported that she was again abducted and subjected to another extensive medical examination. During this abduction, the aliens apparently removed ova. She suggested that her young son was abducted as well. According to Jordan, her son would become another victim of repeated alien abductions.

In April 1986 she was abducted once again. She was shown two infants and allowed to name them and hold them. It was almost as if the aliens were attempting to encourage a mother-child bond. Although she was shown only two small children, she was told that there were nine all together.

Abducted to an Alien Base:

JULY 1987

Location: Tucson, Arizona

Witnesses: Christa Tilton

Encounter Type: Abduction

Craft Type: Unknown

Alien Type: Gray, humanoid, human

Alien Characteristics: One alien, "the doctor," was very human in appearance. Others were described as small gray aliens with big heads, big black eyes, and very thin bodies.

Home World: Unknown

Sources: "I Was Held Captive in an Underground Alien Base," by Christa Tilton in *UFO Universe,* April-May 1991.

Reliability: 4

Narrative: Tilton's story is not unlike that of many others who have been abducted. At age ten, while visiting her aunt's house in Tucson, she was walking down a road when she saw a huge orange ball of fire fall to the ground. Moments later she encountered a small gray being with whom she exchanged rocks. She then lost consciousness and awoke on a table. She saw someone standing over her and was told that she would always remember him as "the doctor."

She was examined while on the craft. The beings took skin scrapings and used a needle or probe to examine the interior of her abdomen. Tilton also felt something sharp in her ear and reported additional tests and examinations during that first abduction.

Over the years, Tilton described other abductions, all with a somewhat similar theme. Like Debbie Jordan, she believed she was impregnated by the aliens, but during an abduction in New Orleans in 1971, the fetus was removed.

The one abduction that seems to separate Tilton from the rest took place in July 1987. Under hypnotic regression, she recalled driving into the desert until she saw a craft sitting on a hill. There were two alien beings waiting for her, and although she locked the doors of her car, they apparently unlocked them. She fought with the beings but was dragged to the craft. Once inside, she was given something to drink, and the next thing she knew, she was being led out of the craft, which was outside a cavern.

Tilton was then escorted into an underground base that she now believes is in the area of Dulce, New Mexico. She was taken into the cavern, where she was forced to go through a long, rigorous security check. She was then led through several levels and given several security checks. At one point her guide argued with some of the guards, but Tilton wasn't able to learn what the fuss was about.

While in the underground facility, she was again examined by the aliens. When the examination ended, the tour continued down to level six. She was not allowed inside because, according to the escorts, things on that level might have upset her, and she might

204

have seen something she couldn't comprehend. The aliens turned and began to walk her back to level one.

When they returned her to her car, she drove to her aunt's house and went to bed without waking either her aunt or her best friend. The next morning her friend noticed some long red scratches on her back that were the result of the struggle to stay away from the alien craft.

Tilton's abductions continue to this day. She often lectures about her experiences as an abductee.

The Gulf Breeze Case:

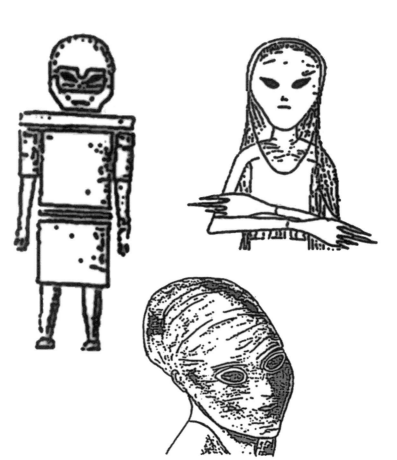

Location: Gulf Breeze, Florida

Witnesses: Ed Walters
Frances Walters

Encounter Type: CE-III, abduction

Craft Type: Disc-shaped vessel with double row of windows

Alien Type: Humanoid

Alien Characteristics: The creatures were described as 4-foot-tall humanoids with big black eyes. They wore helmets with transparent material at eye level that apparently allowed them to see.

Home World: Unknown

Sources: *The Gulf Breeze Sightings: The Most Astounding Multiple UFO Sightings in U.S. History* and *UFO Abductions in Gulf Breeze,* by Ed and Frances Walters; *UFOs in the 1980s,* by Jerry Clark; *Revelations,* by Jacques Vallee; *Alien Contact,* by Timothy Good; *The UFO Encyclopedia,* by John Spencer.

Reliability: 0

Narrative: Although Ed Walters had seen and photographed many UFOs, it wasn't until December 2, 1987, that he first claimed to have seen the creatures from them. He awoke that night when he heard a baby crying. Although there were no babies in either of the neighbors' houses or his own, Walters was upset. He then heard voices speaking Spanish and talking about the crying baby. Walters, carrying a .32-caliber pistol, checked the house and the yard, accompanied by his wife. Out in back, he saw the UFO descending rapidly. It hesitated about 100 feet above the pool, then drifted a short distance before stopping.

Walters retreated to the house with his wife. What he would later refer to as the "UFO voice" commanded that he "Step forward now."

As he had done on previous occasions, Walters grabbed his Polaroid camera and took it, along with his pistol, out the door. Near the pool in his backyard, he took a picture, but when the flash went off, he felt exposed. He ran back into the house. From the kitchen he and his wife watched the UFO vanish. When it was gone, the hum inside his head faded.

Back in bed, Walters said he heard the dog bark once, which he said was unusual. Walters again got up and, carrying both his pistol and his camera, walked to the French doors, sure that he would see the UFO again. Instead, when he opened the curtains, he saw, just inches from him, a 4-foot-tall humanoid with big black eyes. It was wearing a helmet with transparent material at eye level.

During his other UFO experiences Walters seemed to have remained calm enough to take multiple photographs of the craft, but this time he forgot about the camera in his hand. He screamed in surprise, jumped back, and tripped. Walters raised his pistol, thinking he would fire if the creature tried to enter the house, but he never thought to take a picture.

Walters finally got to his feet and then struggled to unlock the door. He put down his pistol and camera. The creature retreated,

208

but was no more than 20 feet away. Walters was sure that he could capture it, but as he opened the door and attempted to step out, he was struck by the blue beam. His foot seemed to be nailed to the floor. As the beam lifted his leg, Walters grabbed the door-jamb for balance. His wife, Frances, grabbed him and pulled on him. Both saw the UFO about 50 feet above the backyard.

With the UFO still hovering, Walters, now free of the blue beam, again grabbed his camera and shot a picture of the UFO. He didn't manage to photograph the alien being, but had the presence of mind to take still another picture of the craft. He saw the object shoot out another blue beam. Walters believed this was meant to pick up the creature, maybe to beam it aboard.

According to Walters's later writings, this was not his only contact with alien beings. Hypnotic regression sessions were arranged through local Mutual UFO Network members with Dr. Dan C. Overlade, a forensic psychologist who specialized in clinical hypnosis. It was thought that the hypnosis would unlock Ed Walters's repressed memories.

During a number of hypnotic regression sessions, Walters told of series of abductions that began, apparently, when he was seventeen years old. The first experience revolves around a large black dog that tracked him as he rode his bike to the store. The frightening animal waited for him and then matched his speed as Walters tried to outrace it on his bike. That night he experienced a belief that something was in the house with him and that it had jumped up on his bed.

Under hypnosis, after having discussed the abductions with Overlade, Walters was reluctant to "see" any of those long-ago events. According to Walters, however, his mind slipped from that event to another that occurred in May 1988 after he had taken many of the photographs he offered as proof of his experiences.

During that first session Walters seemed to refuse to explore the events around that incident, but he did slip forward in time, remembering an abduction that had taken place on May 1, 1988.

Walters described some kind of rod being forced into his nose, causing him pain.

Under hypnosis, still talking about the May 1 event, he remembered lying on the floor in a small room that was covered with a sticky residue. He seemed to know that something was near him and that it was coming toward him. Three beings dressed in the "box-type shields" stood around another creature that wore a gray hood and a pale pink body suit. These creatures were smaller than he, and they carried silver sticks.

He then found himself in a larger room with a table in it. Walters spotted what he believed to be a serial number on the table. He claimed that he later drew the symbols for Budd Hopkins, who said that the symbols were identical to those drawn by other alleged abductees. Those symbols are being withheld for use as controls so that the tales told by new abductees can be checked.

Another being, this one with white hair, entered. Walters was then hit by something, maybe a blue beam, and then "all of a sudden I was sitting on the table."

Walters then described, in a fairly disjointed fashion, what happened next. He did mention a parade of small alien creatures who wore gray body suits which so closely matched their skin tones that Walters found it difficult to see where the suits ended and the skin began.

And he described another creature as small, only about 2 feet tall. It was being carried by others that were a lighter gray. These beings were making him remember parts of his life.

In other sessions with Overlade, Walters described other abductions that spanned his life from his teenage years. In consultation with Hopkins, Walters drew the beings he saw, including a strange-looking alien with strange long-fingered hands and no thumbs. Walters wrote, "Budd [Hopkins] confirmed the thumbless hand with a drawing documented ten years earlier by Leonard Stringfield."

Apparently Walters didn't know that Stringfield later identified the source of that strange-looking hand as part of a hoax—an exhibit of a creature that was supposed to be a mermaid. In his *Status Report VI, UFO Crash/Retrievals: The Inner Sanctum,* released in July 1991, Stringfield published the whole illustration and not the small piece that had been circulating in the UFO community for years.

The Drawing of a Photograph:

Location: Ruby, Arizona

Witnesses: One man, identified only as Sam

Encounter Type: CE-III

Craft Type: Unknown

Alien Type: Humanoid

Alien Characteristics: This being was a small humanoid with normal-size eyes that included pupils. It had an oblong head with a small nose, a small mouth, and a long, angular chin. The skin color was a very light gray. The fingers seemed to have two joints, and there were no noticeable fingernails. The clothing was a light lead gray and had a metallic look.

Home World: Unknown

Sources: "People in focus . . .," in *UFO* magazine

Reliability: 5

Narrative: Ron Quinn sketched, from a photograph, the alien creature that his sixty-six-year-old friend, identified only as Sam, saw. According to Quinn, Sam was taking pictures of Indian ruins in a remote area when he heard a swishing sound followed by a loud boom. Twenty minutes later, after reaching an outcropping of rock, Sam saw a small creature, which he thought at first was a child. As the creature turned toward him, Sam realized it was an alien and shot one picture of it. The being then turned and fled, and although Sam gave chase, the little man got away.

Sam had the photograph developed at a local drugstore. Quinn seems to have been the only one who saw it. He suggested that Sam sell it to a magazine or tabloid newspaper for as much as he could. So far that hasn't happened.

Aliens Down Under:

AUGUST 8, 1993

Location: Belgrave, Victoria, Australia

Witnesses: Kelly Cahill (age 27)

Encounter Type: Abduction

Craft Type: Round with windows

Alien Type: Humanoid

Alien Characteristics: The creatures were 7 feet tall and black. They had thin arms and legs and glowing red eyes that resembled the eyes of flies.

Home World: Unknown

Sources: "An Extraordinary Encounter in the Dandenong Foothills," by Bill Chalker in the *International UFO Reporter,* September-October 1994.

Reliability: 5

Narrative: Cahill and her husband were driving home when they saw a craft hovering above the road in front of them. Not far away, they came to a light so bright that Kelly raised her hand to shield her eyes. A moment later she asked her husband what had happened, but when they reached home, they realized they were about an hour later than they should have been. She also found a triangular mark on her navel.

Later she remembered that she and her husband had been driving along a curved road. The craft they had thought was sitting on the road was actually off to one side. Cahill had told her husband to stop the car, and both got out. The huge object turned out to be a black creature. Near it she saw others. A group of the creatures began to move toward her while another group headed toward a second car that had stopped. Cahill believed the beings were evil. She heard her husband telling them to let go, and then she was sick. She screamed at the creatures and found herself back in her car.

Like so many others, Cahill had a series of dreams about the encounter. She believed that one of the creatures bent over her as if to kiss her on the stomach.

A Closing Comment or
Two on Abductions

Stories of abduction by alien beings is not a new phenomenon. We can go back to the tales of elves and fairies abducting humans to do their bidding, and myths in which the Greek and Roman gods abducted humans for their sexual pleasure. Abduction by ETs has been widely publicized since 1966 when John Fuller chronicled the abduction of Betty and Barney Hill. Since then more and more people have come forward with similar tales.

Abduction researchers have been intrigued by the similarities in the reports given by people who claim to have been abducted. Notable researchers such as Budd Hopkins, Dr. John Mack, and David Jacobs write about the abduction phenomenon and the gray aliens. They often suggest that if there is nothing to these stories, then why do the witnesses describe the same types of alien beings even though they have never met to discuss the subject.

We have interviewed over 150 alleged abductees, and, yes, there are similarities, but there are also some major dissimilarities. One major difference is that nearly all of the abductees recall more than one type of alien; some recall as many as seven types.

Kathy Davis [Debbie Jordan] is the young lady who was featured in *Intruders,* by Budd Hopkins. The abductions in that book focus on the gray aliens, but in an interview with us, Davis told us about the balls of light and a human blond alien with a catlike eye that moved when he spoke.

Licia Davidson, a lifelong abductee, has gone so far as to divide the aliens into categories. The first is the classic gray, 3 to 4 feet in height with pasty gray skin. Davidson said that these are the workers. The second category is made up of tans. They have an appearance similar to the grays but with a more angular face. They stand about 5 feet tall and seem to function as the medical division of the alien troop. In the third group are the 5- to 6-foot-tall grays. They seem to be the officers, or leaders, of the aliens with whom Licia had contact. The fourth alien is the "big boss" whom Licia has given the name "Grace Jones." Licia has always had the feeling that this alien is female. The big boss stands about 7 feet tall, is very dark skinned, and always wears a hooded cloak. The fifth and last of the aliens that Licia has encountered are of the human or "Nordic" form. They took much like us, with the males standing about 6 feet tall and the females about 5 feet tall. They have very bronze skin and blond hair.

Licia is not alone in her description of the alien visitors. At least four other abductees that we have interviewed have described five to six types of aliens, and they are very similar to Licia's except for color and clothing. Jesse Long, a lifetime abductee, describes a reptoid alien that came to him when he was a child. As Jesse grew into adulthood many different types of aliens came to him, either alone or in groups. The one standout alien, which Jesse has labeled "the calming factor" is a 7-foot-tall white alien covered with a veil.

Matthew Stoic has been visited by all types of gray aliens, from short ones in uniform to tall ones. He also has been visited by an 8-foot-tall and very spiritual human. Kim Carlsberg has also been visited by both the gray types and a 7-foot-tall white alien.

We have reported on the Barney and Betty Hill case, but we haven't stressed that Betty Hill's description of the aliens has evolved over the years. Originally they had noses that she suggested rivaled that of Jimmy Durante. In later years, however, the description changed until it was closer to that of the gray. But if we go by the original testimony taken by Dr. Benjamin Simon and the notes that Betty Hill kept, we see that the aliens who abducted her were not the classic grays.

Hickson and Parker, the men taken during the wave of 1973, didn't mention the grays at all. Again, we have a description of a creature that is more robotic in nature with legs that seemed to be fused together.

Five days after Hickson-Parker, Pat Roach produced a drawing of an alien that seemed to match that made by Barney Hill a decade earlier. Under hypnosis, her drawing changed but not into the gray of the classic abduction. Instead, like so many others whose descriptions are often ignored, she drew a creature that had pupils in round eyes that weren't much larger than human eyes. She also gave the being a nose rather than the two holes often associated with the gray of later abductions.

A year after the Hickson-Parker abduction and that of Pat Roach, the Avis family was abducted. The creatures described by both John and Elaine Avis do not fit into the classic gray category. In fact, both abductees reported that the work was done by a hairy little beast that is more reminiscent of a werewolf than of an alien from space.

One type of alien creature seems to have been almost universally ignored: the reptilian being that looks like an advanced predatory dinosaur. These aliens stand 5 to 7 feet tall and are often said to have green skin and thick tails. They are not unlike the velociraptors from *Jurassic Park*. The reptoids, as they are sometimes called, are emotional aliens. They are the most active and seem to be highly sexual. They are also highly technical, and they seem to relate to children and women better than do the grays and other reported creatures. They are also the most violent of the alien abductors. One witness recalled seeing two reptoids in a fight in which one of them was killed. Others report sexual assaults that go far beyond the reproductive experimentation carried out by other alien groups. In fact, there is a midwestern support group for those who claim to have been raped by reptoids.

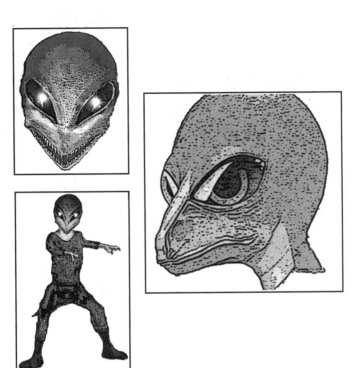

Although Budd Hopkins has stated that 85 percent of all abductions are performed by the "classic" 3-foot-tall grays, we have found that this is not the case. To suggest such a standardization of the descriptions of the alien creatures is to miss the rich tradition and history of the phenomenon. In fact, it is almost as if the researchers are engaging in wishful thinking. They are trying to make some sense out of data that seem to have no sense. Variety rather than standardization seems to be the norm here.

Skeptics have claimed that *Close Encounters of the Third Kind,* the Steven Spielberg movie, is responsible for setting, in the minds of many, the "proper" image of an alien being. While we certainly have found a variety, we have also seen the beginning of the standardization. It could be that the film did influence the way witnesses of the 1990s have perceived aliens. Yes, small aliens were mentioned prior to that film, but once it was released, more of the witnesses were using the aliens in it as a basis for their claims. The question that has to be asked here is whether the movie was influenced by the research being conducted or whether the movie influenced the witnesses. It is the classic chicken-and-egg argument.

In our research—and again we stress that we have personally interviewed more than 150 men and women who claim abduction—we have found over 100 different kinds of alien visitors. We have found the grays, too, often in the same cases with other types of creatures. And we find that the grays are beginning to appear more often. To ignore the variety of alien descriptions is to do a disservice to UFO research. We must gather all the data and not just those that fit into the patterns we are developing.

Part IV

The Photographs

As we were assembling this work, we noticed something odd: After more than fifty years of UFO sightings and landing reports, we had hundreds of descriptions of UFO occupants but only a handful of photographs. In a country that is full of cameras, from the Instamatic to the Polaroid to the video camera, it seems that no one thinks to take pictures of the creatures from the flying saucers. That strikes us as extremely strange.

We have hundreds of pictures from the Civil War, which ended more than a century ago. We have movie footage from the First World War, which ended more than three quarters of a century ago. And of course we have color footage from the Second World War, which ended half a century ago. But of the occupants of flying saucers, we have virtually nothing.

In today's society we have videotape of everything—aircraft falling out of the sky, parachutists whose chutes haven't opened, traffic accidents, explosions, and armed robberies. If there is an event today, someone, somewhere, will videotape it.

So what about photographs of UFO occupants? We have some lousy pictures taken decades ago. We have photographs that are in dispute because of the tales told about them. We have photographs that are so poor as to be useless. We have photographs that are clearly hoaxes, and we have shots of wax and rubber special effects dummies made for science-fiction movies. And even when we can identify them as such, we hear how those who made the movies actually used the real thing as the basis for their special effects.

The point is, there are some pictures, and to the best of our knowledge, no one has ever attempted to assemble them in a single work. The reason for that might be that they are all of such poor quality that no one really cares. Also, there is no corroboration for them, the background of the witnesses is less than sterling, and there is no way to verify their validity.

As we conducted our research, we found nothing to suggest that any of the following pictures are authentic. The facts around them seem to argue against their authenticity. For example, one of them is said to have been taken in 1949 or the early 1950s in Mexico or Mexico City, but anyone looking at the photo would conclude that it was, in fact, taken in Europe.

Other photographs were taken by the contactees. Again, we have no way to corroborate them. Each one is out of focus, overexposed, or otherwise unclear. It would be nice to have a solid shot of a landed disc with little grays standing around it. Instead we have photographs in which there is no recognizable terrain, no skyscrapers in the background, and no humans anywhere. They could be shots of miniatures, of humans in costume, or of models. The quality of the photographs is so poor that we just can't tell.

Keeping in mind the fact that the reliability of these pictures is questionable, we have gathered them together here and have provided the facts accompanying their appearance, so that you can assess their value for yourselves.

Alien Autopsy Photos:

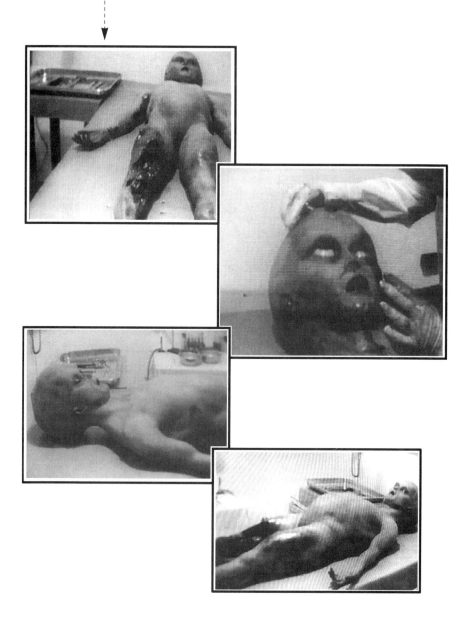

Location: Near Socorro, New Mexico

Witnesses: An unknown military photographer variously identified as Jack Barnett, Jack Barrett, or Jack Snow.

Encounter Type: CE-III

Craft Type: Unknown

Alien Type: Humanoid

Alien Characteristics: This creature has black lenses over large eyes, low-set ears, a large bald head, thick arms and legs, a distended belly, and a large chest.

Home World: Unknown

Sources: "Alien Autopsy," Fox-TV

Reliability: 0

Narrative: Although this film was originally promoted as a record of the autopsy of one of the creatures killed in the crash of an alien spacecraft outside of Roswell, New Mexico, it soon became apparent that it was not. The crash supposedly took place more than a month earlier near the west New Mexican town of Socorro.

The photographer claimed that he was in Washington, D.C., when the call came to rush out to New Mexico. He landed at Wright Field and then flew on to Roswell. There he switched to a car and drove the rest of the way to the crash site. Apparently no one had examined the crash site or begun an autopsy until the photographer arrived to record the event.

He was able, at that time, to film a preliminary autopsy performed in either a tent or a barn. The lighting was bad, and the film is of little value. Almost nothing can be seen. Others have suggested that the film once included scenes of the debris field filled with soldiers and equipment attempting to recover the wreckage. Some people claim that then President Harry Truman could be seen walking in one missing scene. That footage has never been shown publicly, however, and it appears now that it doesn't exist.

About a month later the cameraman was told to film an autopsy of one of the aliens that was held in the Dallas–Fort Worth area. The lighting was much better, and a great deal of detail could be seen. According to a clock on the wall, the autopsy lasted about two hours.

The validity of the autopsy footage has been argued since it was first shown publicly in May 1995. At that time, Kent Jeffery, the driving force behind the Roswell Initiative, saw a document designed to force the release of the files about the case and proclaimed the autopsy to be a fake.

Other researchers have made similar claims. The most valid ones seem to be based on the reluctance of the film's owners to allow testing on the film to date it. Kodak has said they could tell a great deal if they were allowed to examine a long stretch of film. This would be a nondestructive analysis.

Kodak has also asked to have one frame of the film with the

alien body on it for a chemical analysis. While such tests will not prove definitively that the film is authentic, they would go a long way toward establishing its authenticity. To this point, the owners of the film have refused to meet the conditions or make any of the film with the alien on it available. They have provided short segments to various researchers, but there is nothing on those short segments to suggest that the film is part of the autopsy footage. In other words, the owners of the film have done nothing to validate it. On the contrary, they have done everything possible to prevent its validation.

The cameraman's statement, released later, seems to tell the story not in an American voice but in a British voice. This has been explained somewhat weakly by proponents who suggest that the British secretary who transcribed the tape changed it to British dialect from the original American.

The point here, however, is that the tale and the autopsy footage are highly questionable. Nothing has been offered to suggest that they are authentic, but a great deal of evidence suggests the film is fraudulent.

ALIEN AUTOPSY PHOTOS

The *Penthouse* Photographs
of Roswell:

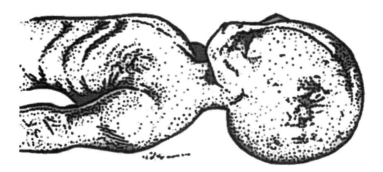

Location: Roswell, New Mexico

Witnesses: An unidentified daughter of a German scientist

Encounter Type: CE-III

Craft Type: Unknown

Alien Type: Human

Alien Characteristics: This alien has a large bald head, large dark eyes, a thin body, and thin limbs.

Home World: Unknown

Sources: *Penthouse,* September 1996; *Roswell,* a Showtime movie, 1994.

Reliability: 0

Narrative: Bob Guccioni, publisher of *Penthouse* magazine, claims that he has found photographs that come from the real autopsy film of the Roswell aliens, and not the fake that was broadcast in 1995. Keith Farrel, one of those who edited the now defunct *Omni* magazine, wrote about the photographs that had been received from a woman who claimed her father was a German scientist working in New Mexico in 1947 as a member of the team that was assembled to investigate the crash. She had been entrusted with a small segment of the film but was told never to reveal what was on it, or even its existence, to anyone. If someone learned of the film's existence, it could mean her death.

Guccione was quoted in a wire service story as saying, "I am absolutely 100 percent convinced" of the authenticity of the photographs. He appeared on CNBC to show the magazine and the pictures, telling the audience there was no doubt that he had the real thing.

In fact, to demonstrate the credibility of the photographs, Guccione noted that *Omni* had organized a team of highly qualified experts who had been studying UFOs. Guccione implied that all of the experts had inspected the pictures and were impressed with them.

The photographs show a badly injured being about 4 feet tall, thin, with a large head, and it seems, large eyes. The creature is clearly not human, though it is humanoid. If the pictures are as authentic as Guccione claims, he has broken the story of the millennium.

But those of us who have seen *Roswell,* the Showtime original movie, have already seen this particular alien. There is no doubt that it is one of the four or five special effects models created for the movie.

Guccione, during the CNBC program, was asked about that possibility, but said that he believed the filmmakers had access to some of the same pictures. They modeled their special effects creation after the real thing.

We provided technical assistance for that film, however, and we know this isn't true. Paul Davids, the executive producer of the film, has said repeatedly that he is 100 percent sure the Guccione photographs are of one of the special effects models. Asked if the movie people could have used the real thing as a model, he told me, "Absolutely not."

Someone misrepresented the pictures to Guccione and convinced him that they show the real thing. If you wonder how someone outside the film crew, the actors, the director, or anyone else on the set could have gotten pictures of one of the models, you don't have to go far. It is clear that the pictures Guccione published were taken in the International UFO Museum, at the small display they have set up. it is clear from the injuries on the head that this is the model that has been photographed.

Another Part of the Roswell Story:

JULY 5, 1947

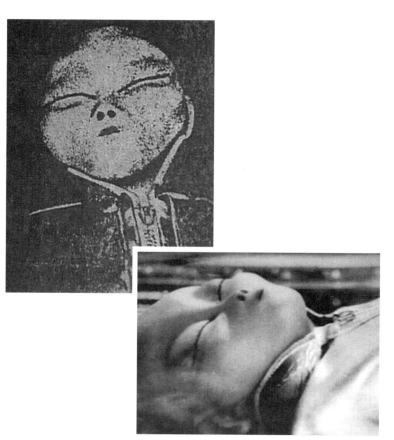

Location: Plains of San Agustin, New Mexico

Witnesses: Unidentified

Encounter Type: CE-III

Craft Type: Unknown

Alien Type: Humanoid

Alien Characteristics: These beings had big eyes, small mouths, and small noses.

Home World: Unknown

Sources: *UFO Universe.*

Reliability: 0

Narrative: The story, as it is most often told, is that the late Dr. J. Allen Hynek, former scientific consultant to the air force's Project Blue Book, somehow got copies of pictures of alien bodies. Hynek supposedly gave the pictures to the late Dr. Felix Ziegel who lectured in astronomy and physics. The pictures first surfaced in a Russian publication, which suggested that they were photos of a model. Others, who were promoting the photographs as authentic, said that it was of a model, but the model was based on real photographs.

Antonio Huneeus, who had heard parts of the story, decided to follow it as far as he could. He learned that a Canadian named Linda Corrivau had experienced a close encounter. She'd had a sculptor create the model based on her sighting report. It had been displayed in 1977 in Canada, and hundreds of people had photographed it. According to her, she invited Hynek to Canada to see the creation.

Once again it was suggested that the mock-up was modeled after a real being. And once again it was suggested that the U.S. Army had possession of the real thing, an actual extraterrestrial being, and was preserving it on ice.

There is no doubt, however, that these photographs, which have been circulated far and wide and which are sometimes blamed on Allen Hynek, are of a wax model.

The Tomato Man:

Location: Laredo, Texas

Witnesses: Unidentified military photographer

Encounter Type: CE-III

Craft Type: Disc

Alien Type: Humanoid

Alien Characteristics: This was a large being with a bald head.

Home World: Unknown

Sources: *Mysteries of the Unknown: The UFO Phenomenon,* Time-Life Books.

Reliability: 0

Narrative: A newly formed Maryland UFO group received two photographs from a source that asked them what they could tell about it. They suggested it showed the body of a pilot killed in the crash of a small plane. The source wrote back telling them that it was the body of an alien killed when its ship crashed in Texas.

Armed with the negatives from the source, the UFO investigators contacted experts at Kodak, who determined that the negative was old enough to have been made in the 1940s. That didn't mean the picture showed a dead alien, only that there was nothing on the negative to suggest a hoax.

The photographs were released to the press in 1980 with the suggestion that here, for the first time, were legitimate pictures proving not only that aliens had visited Earth but that one ship had crashed, providing the U.S. government with all the evidence it needed: flying saucers were real and were here.

There were those who suggested the pictures were faked. One man wrote, "Universally condemned as hoaxes by skeptics and establishment alike, the photos remain unidentified."

We give him the benefit of the doubt. He probably wrote those words before he had closely examined the pictures. In fact, even the poorest quality pictures showed, under the body of the dead pilot, a pair of clearly terrestrial eyeglasses.

The Monkey Man:

Circa 1949

Location: Mexico City

Witnesses: Unidentified

Encounter Type: CE-III

Craft Type: Unknown

Alien Type: Humanoid

Alien Characteristics: This small, slender-bodied being stood about 27 inches tall and had long, slender arms.

Home World: Unknown

Reliability: 0

Narrative: Information about this picture is sketchy at best, and more than one version is available. It seems that several discs were seen in the Monument Valley on March 21, 1949. Not long after that, similar craft were seen discharging small cylinders over

Mexico City. A small creature was inside one of them. He was captured and turned over to the proper authorities.

Although it is claimed that the picture was taken in Mexico, the human subjects' clothing looks to be European. The picture has never been authenticated.

Army Escorts a Small Creature:

Location: West Germany

Witnesses: John Quinn

Encounter Type: CE-III

Craft Type: Unknown

Alien Type: Humanoid

Alien Characteristics: This short humanoid creature was wearing a helmet with breathing apparatus.

Home World: Unknown

Sources: *The Roswell Incident*, by Charles Berlitz and William Moore.

Reliability: 0

Narrative: No report of this sighting, merely the picture, which is supposed to be of an alien creature in the custody of two American MPs. The creature is reportedly the survivor of a UFO, but no details about the crash are available, nor do we know the date of the event or the identities of the two MPs.

Like so many other photographs, this one first surfaced in Europe, where an American GI supposedly bought it for a dollar. The unidentified GI turned the picture over to John Quinn on May 22, 1950, but provided no additional information. Without that, and with no way to corroborate its authenticity, this becomes just another picture that has no provenance and therefore must be disregarded.

Alien in a Space Suit:

JULY 1952

Location: Berina Mountains, Italy

Witnesses: Gianpietro Monguzzi

Encounter Type: CE-III

Craft Type: Disc

Alien Type: Humanoid

Alien Characteristics: This small, stocky creature was wearing a space suit that obscured its face and head.

Home World: Unknown

Sources: *What We Really Know About Flying Saucers,* by Otto Binder.

Reliability: 2

Narrative: Gianpietro Monguzzi, an Italian engineer, while on vacation with his wife in the Berina Mountains came upon a landed saucer. He took a series of pictures of the craft and, when the pictures were developed and enlarged, discovered that he had photographed one of the aliens. The pictures have been rejected as faked because no corroborative testimony is available.

A Contactee's Photograph:

Location: Eastern United States

Witnesses: Howard Menger

Encounter Type: Contact

Craft Type: Disc

Alien Type: Humanoid

Alien Characteristics: The creature in this photograph looks remarkably human.

Home World: Venus

Sources: *The Encyclopedia of UFOs,* by Ronald Story.

Reliability: 2

Narrative: Menger, who claimed many contacts with the beings from other worlds, managed to take a few photographs of them.

Although he claims that his contacts began in 1932, he mentioned nothing about them until the 1950s. He says that he traveled to many different worlds, but aside from his photographs, he has provided no evidence to prove it. And all of the photographs were taken on Earth.

The Police Chief Photo:

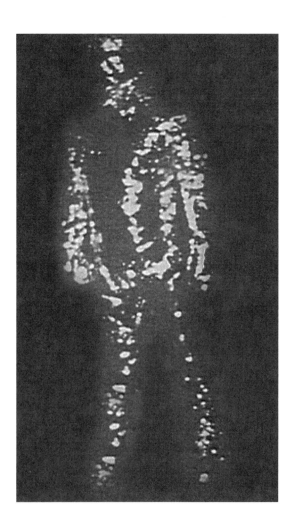

Location: Falkville, Alabama

Witnesses: Police Chief Jeffrey Greenhaw (age 26)

Encounter Type: CE-III

Craft Type: Unknown

Alien Type: Humanoid

Alien Characteristics: This photo shows a tall creature in a bright silvery suit. It has the stature and appearance of a human in a silvery fire-fighting suit.

Home World: Unknown

Sources: *High Strangeness: UFOs from 1960 Through 1979*, by Jerome Clark.

Reliability: 5

Narrative: Greenhaw, the chief of police and, in fact, the only member of the Falkville Police Department, claimed that he received a phone call at about 10:00 P.M. telling him that a UFO had landed nearby. Greenhaw drove toward the location and came upon a figure, about 5½ feet tall, standing in the road, dressed in a silver suit. Greenhaw stopped his patrol car and tried to speak to the creature while taking pictures of it. As it began to advance, he turned on the rotating red light on top of his car, causing the creature to flee. Greenhaw gave chase in his car, but the alien outran him when he lost traction on the loose gravel of the dirt road.

Within weeks of the sighting, his report, and the national attention given to his photographs, Greenhaw's wife left him, his trailer home burned, and he lost his job. Later he would claim that government officials had shown him documents proving that his sighting was valid, but they refused to release the papers to him. Greenhaw was forced to leave the state, according to him, because of pressure by outsiders.

NICAP investigator Marion Webb put on a fire-fighting suit that had the same sort of silvery surface. Photographs of that suit look remarkably like those taken by Greenhaw. Ground Saucer Watch, another civilian UFO organization, concluded that the photographs were a hoax designed to take advantage of the publicity surrounding the wave of sightings in 1973.

Conclusions by investigators suggested that Greenhaw and a young friend had invented the tale because of the number of sightings that were being reported. The pictures were taken about a week after national news Charles Hickson and Calvin Parker made by claiming they had been abducted. Greenhaw has steadfastly maintained that he was not a participant in a hoax.

Captured Creature:

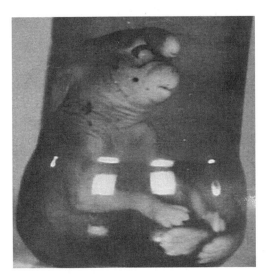

5 Ptas. SPAIN

25¢. U.S.A.

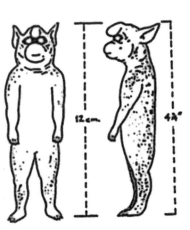

12 cm.

4½"

Location: Near Gerona, in Catalonia, Spain

Witnesses: Unidentified

Encounter Type: CE-III

Craft Type: Unknown

Alien Type: Tiny humanoid

Alien Characteristics: This alien was only about 5 inches tall and had pointed ears, yellow eyes, and blue skin.

Home World: Unknown

Sources: *Who's Who in Spanish Ufology*, by Antonio Hueeus, in *UFO Universe.*

Reliability: 2

Narrative: This tiny creature was captured by two couples who were having a picnic. When the witnesses investigated the sound of strange laughter, they found and captured the little being. According to them, it was quite docile, emitted sounds like laughter, and seemed to be intelligent. They kept it for four days, but it refused to eat. It died shortly after the capture.

The body was said to be made of "animal" cells, and Dr. John Altshuler, who saw the photographs, told Huneeus that it was not the fetus of a cow or a pig. The creature is being preserved by Spanish ufologist Angel Gordon.

Part V

The Database

The Wave of 1954

A massive but often overlooked wave of sightings took place in 1954, not in the United States but in Western Europe and South America. During that year dozens of witnesses reported seeing creatures emerging from spacecraft to collect samples or to interact with humans.

For the most part, however, this wave has been ignored in the United States. Maybe we just couldn't accept the tales of alien creatures walking the Earth. Maybe, because of the tales told by the contactees—George Adamski, George Van Tassel, Howard Menger, and others—we just didn't believe the occupant reports. We'd already heard some tales of the alien beings and those made no sense to us. We lumped the occupant sightings in with the contactee reports.

But we were willing to listen to tales of spacecraft being seen in the sky. In some cases we would even listen to reports of craft sighted on the ground. Too often, however, we ignored the tales about the creatures who piloted the craft. These reports were treated with even more scorn than the run-of-the-mill flying saucer sightings.

One point must be made here. During the wave of 1954 there were many good sightings of spacecraft in the sky. On September 21, for example, thousands of people in Rome, including military and civilian pilots and high-ranking government officials, watched a cigar-shaped craft maneuver over the city. More importantly, the object was tracked on radar. Here was just the sort of case that skeptics often demanded, yet because it happened in Italy, it has remained virtually unknown in this country. Unfortunately, the Rome incident was neither a landing-trace case nor an occupant sighting report. Like most UFO sightings, it was just a report of a strange craft seen in the sky. Despite the added corroboration of radar tracking, this was essentially just a sighting report.

We have rejected occupant reports and landing cases because, according to some authorities, there was a lack of good corroboration for them. There was no physical evidence proving the landing had taken place.

The major exception was, of course, the Roswell crash case. There we did have high-ranking military officers as well as civilian authorities suggesting that the crash had taken place and that the occupants' bodies had been recovered.

But in Europe and South America in 1954, this situation changed: corroboration and evidence were suddenly available. On September 10, 1954, Maruis Dewilde was walking his dog along the railroad tracks at night near Valenciennes, France, when he saw a dark mass sitting on the roadbed. Not far from the craft were two small, wide-shouldered creatures who wore huge helmets. Dewilde wanted to walk over to them, but a bright light from the craft paralyzed him. The creatures hurried back to the craft, there was a loud whistling sound, and the object lifted into the night sky. Later examination showed depressions in the railroad ties that suggested a craft weighing 30 tons had been standing there.

On October 11, 1954, near La Croix Durade, France, a glowing object was seen lifting from a field. It disappeared in seconds, leaving flattened grass and other traces behind.

On December 19, 1954, near Valencia, Venezuela, a jockey, running in the cool of the morning, saw a disc-shaped object hovering just off the ground. Several small creatures were loading boulders into it, just as American astronauts, years later, would collect rocks on the moon. When the creatures spotted the jockey, they turned a purple ray on him that paralyzed him while they scrambled back into their craft. Later investigations revealed strange tracks on the ground.

Also interesting is the number of separate reports in which witnesses claim to have been paralyzed by a ray from the aliens. The jockey said the creatures paralyzed him with a purple ray. Dewilde, who saw the craft on the railroad, was also paralyzed. As we check out the sightings, we find many others in which the witnesses were paralyzed. Dr. Henri Robert was paralyzed in his car after the engine was stalled by a low-flying disc. A man standing close to a reddish disc suggested that he too was paralyzed.

In a number of cases the creatures seem to have been trying to abduct the witnesses. In Brazil, two boys who had been hunting were attacked by four small hairy creatures that tried to drag one of the boys off. In Venezuela, Jesus Paz walked into some bushes and began to scream. When his friends came to his aid, they saw a hairy creature running away.

It needs to be pointed out here that these witnesses were able to fight off the alien creatures. That is in odd conflict with our modern reports in which the victims are unable to resist the alien abduction attempts.

We can also look at a case from Santo Amaro, Brazil, in which a taxi driver found a landed disc with an open door. When he walked in and was spotted by three creatures, he found himself backing out of the craft against his will. This suggests that some of the alien beings have been able to control human movements.

Some people claim that the wave of 1954 introduced a number of new concepts into the UFO phenomenon, but it didn't really. All of these types of reports had been made before. This wave, however, did include a large number of occupant reports, landing reports, and descriptions of alien beings.

Though marked by peaks in France and South America, this wave actually began in Germany. By mid-August 1954 the number of sightings had begun to increase in France, where huge peaks were reached in late September and October. By September the sightings were coming from all over Western Europe and extended south into Africa. Many of these sightings were merely reports of objects in the sky, but there were dozens in which the craft were seen on the ground.

If we follow the standard technique of looking for similarities among the reports, we quickly see that the beings were said to have worn diving suits and helmets with tubes extending down into backpacks, and the use of a paralyzing ray is often mentioned. On November 11, 1954, near Isola, Italy, a farmer watched as a cigar-shaped craft landed in a field. Three small creatures exited. The farmer, convinced that they had come to steal his rabbits, ran for his rifle. As he raised it, it grew so heavy that he dropped it. Then he became paralyzed.

We must remember, however, that these sightings did not take place in a vacuum. Just as the American press had done in 1947 and 1952, the European newspapers carried the stories. Jacques Vallee, writing in *Challenge to Science,* commented that many reports that were not mentioned by researchers could be found in the newspapers, which often carried the tales complete with witnesses' names and addresses. In other words, a great deal of information was provided by the newspapers, but no organization existed to investigate it.

Vallee reports that the French wave had begun to slow by November, but the number of reports increased in South America, Africa, Asia, and Australia. This demonstrates the worldwide presence of the UFO phenomenon. Even though we believe that the vast majority of sightings take place in the United States, the simple fact is that sightings in other parts of the world are rarely reported in the United States. Newspapers and television news reports ignore most of these sightings and consider the reports unreliable. UFO researchers, however, are well aware of the number of sightings coming from other parts of the world.

The 1954 Occupant Database

March 15, 1954, Santa Maria, Brazil: Rubem Hellwig

When Hellwig spotted a football-shaped object landing nearby, he stopped his car and approached it. He saw two creatures near the UFO. They were of average size with brown faces and light hair. One was gathering samples while the other watched, maybe standing guard. They spoke to Hellwig in a language he couldn't understand. Finally they returned to their ship, which took off and disappeared into the distance.

March 16, 1954, Santa Maria, Brazil: Rubem Hellwig

In his second sighting in as many days, Hellwig came across the same ship but different crew members. This time he saw one man and two women. Each of the women had long dark hair, a dark complexion, and large eyes. They told Hellwig they were studying the natural riches of Brazil.

August 23, 1954, Thonon, France

A man approached a landed UFO near which two small creatures were standing. They were dressed in light-colored suits, and they grunted like pigs. Eventually they entered the craft, which glowed brightly and then took off quickly.

September 10, 1954, Mourieras, France

A farmer on his way home saw a man of average height wearing a helmet. The man made friendly gestures, then finally turned away and walked into the forest. A moment later a cigar-shaped craft lifted off.

September 10, 1954, Valenciennes, France: Maruis Dewilde

Dewilde, walking his dog along the railroad tracks at night, noticed a dark mass. Not far away were two small creatures that had wide shoulders and wore huge helmets. Dewilde planned to approach the men, but a bright light from the craft paralyzed him. The creatures returned to the craft, there was a loud whistling noise, and it rose into the sky. An examination of the rail bed revealed depressions on the ties where the object had stood.

September 17, 1954, Cenon, France: Yves David

David was bicycling when he felt a tingling all over his body. He stopped and got off his bike as his headlight went out. In front of him he saw the dark shape of a craft about 10 feet long and 3 feet high. David, the tingling having spread through his body and paralyzed him, watched as a small silhouette moved away from the craft. It approached him, touched him on the shoulder, and then returned to the ship, which gave off a greenish glow, then disappeared. When it was gone, David recovered the use of his limbs.

September 26, 1954, Valence, France

While gathering mushrooms in the woods, a woman saw a small humanoid, which she thought was a scarecrow. It seemed to be wearing a diving suit with a clear helmet. When it began moving toward her, she fled, badly frightened. When she looked back, the creature was gone. A few moments later she heard a loud whistling and saw a disc-shaped object lift from the woods. Evidence of a landing was later found.

September 30, 1954, Marcilly-sur-Vienne, France

Eight construction workers reported seeing a disc-shaped object sitting on the ground. Standing nearby they saw a small humanoid wearing a helmet.

September 30, 1954, Ligescourt, France: Bernard Devoisin and Rene Coudette

Devoisin and Coudette were riding their bicycles when they spotted a glowing orange object sitting on the road. Near it was a small creature in a diving suit. The being returned to the object, which then took off.

October 4, 1954, Poncey, France: Yvette Fourneret

As Fourneret was about to close a window in her home, she saw an object about 10 feet in diameter hovering near a plum tree. Its glow threw a pale light on the tree. She ran next door, and moments later two men armed with shotguns entered the field. They didn't find the object but did discover a hole where soil had been pulled from the ground.

October 4, 1954, Salta, Argentina

A number of children reported seeing three small humanoid creatures with greenish skin.

October 5, 1954, Loctudy, France

A baker was drawing water from a well when he noticed an object he estimated to be 10 feet in diameter sitting on the ground. A small being with a hairy face and large oval eyes approached him and spoke to him in a strange language. The baker called his boss, and they watched as the creature got back into the craft, which then took off quickly.

October 5, 1954, Mertrud, France

A road repairman spotted a strange object sitting on the road. Near it he saw a small hairy creature. The being returned to the craft, which then took off. Traces from the craft were found on the road.

October 9, 1954, Pournoy, France

Four children saw a bright glow from a nearby cemetery. Approaching, they saw an object about 8 feet in diameter standing on three legs. A small creature carrying a bright light exited the craft. It spoke to them, but they couldn't understand it. They finally ran away, and when they looked back, they saw that the object was already in the sky, flying away.

October 9, 1954, Carcassonne, France: Jean Bertrand

Bertrand was driving when he spotted a spherical object sitting on the road in front of him. Through a translucent top, he could see a human-shaped shadow moving. As he approached, the object took off.

October 9, 1954, Rinkerode, Germany

A movie projectionist saw a cigar-shaped craft sitting near the road. Near the object, which gave off a blue light, were four small beings wearing rubber overalls. They had large chests and thin arms and legs, and they seemed to be working on the underside of the object.

October 9, 1954, Lovoux, France

A cyclist saw a small creature carrying a double-beam light, which it used to paralyze the man. The creature walked along the road for a short distance and then disappeared into the forest.

October 11, 1954, Taupignac, France

Three men traveling in a car spotted a disc-shaped craft sitting in a field. Four tiny humanoids were working nearby. When they saw the men, they ran to the disc and shot a beam of light at the men so that they couldn't give chase. The craft then took off.

October 12, 1954, Tehran, Iran

A witness claimed that he clearly saw a creature moving around inside a disc-shaped object that was hovering close to the ground. The being was tiny and dressed in black. When a crowd began to gather, the craft flew away.

October 12, 1954, Lauttey, Morocco

A French engineer saw a creature about 4 feet tall, dressed in a silver suit, entering a disc-shaped object. It took off quickly, disappearing in just seconds.

October 13, 1954, Bourasote, France

Three people saw a reddish disc-shaped craft about 12 feet in diameter. Although the witnesses were not together, they all reported that the being wore a shiny suit and had a large head and enormous eyes. The man closest to the object claimed he was paralyzed, and when the craft finally took off, he was thrown to the ground.

October 14, 1954, Meral, France

A farmer was leaving his home when a glowing ball landed not far from him. It gave off a bright light that illuminated the fields for about 200 yards. As he approached it, he saw a domed disc that appeared to be translucent. Behind the glow he could see a dark shape moving about. Then the light changed from white to red and the object took off at great speed.

October 15, 1954, Toulouse, France

A witness reported that he saw a small creature with large eyes near a small disc-shaped craft.

October 16, 1954, Baillolet, France: Dr. Henri Robert

Robert watched four disc-shaped objects fly over his car. One of them dropped out of the formation, and as it approached the ground, Robert's car stalled and his headlights faded. Robert felt paralyzed as he sat in the car during the whole sighting. A small creature appeared and moved, illuminated by the glow of the craft. When the light went out, he could see nothing. When the craft finally took off, Robert could again move, and he was able to start his car.

October 17, 1954, Isle of Capri, Italy

An artist walking along a road came upon a landed, disc-shaped craft about 15 feet in diameter. Four small creatures dressed in coveralls emerged from it.

October 18, 1954, Doubs, France

A motorcyclist noticed a red glow on the road. She thought nothing of it until, moments later, she saw a figure near the road. It was dressed in a one-piece silver suit and was accompanied by two smaller beings. She continued on but looked back in time to see a round object lifting into the sky

October 18, 1954, Fontenay-Forey, France

A couple watched a cigar-shaped craft as it suddenly dived toward the ground. The couple approached it and saw a being about 3 feet tall. Its eyes seemed to glow orange. Four other witnesses reported watching the red-glowing cigar in flight.

October 18, 1954, Royan, France

A couple watched two ball-shaped objects that appeared to be joined by a bright beam of light. When the light went out, the two objects landed separately. A small creature got out of each craft and entered the other craft. Both ships then took off and flew away.

October 21, 1954, Shrewsbury, England: Jennie Roestenburg

Roestenburg and her two children watched an aluminum-colored disc with transparent panels. Inside they saw two men with white skin and long hair. They wore skintight suits and helmets.

October 27, 1954, Les Jonquets-de-Livet, France

A farmer watched a cigar-shaped object with lights on both ends as it landed in a nearby field. He didn't investigate then, but later, with a group of people, he sighted the object again. The witnesses saw two small creatures in silver suits near the object, which later took off silently.

November 2, 1954, Santo Amaro, Brazil

A taxi driver saw a large glowing object sitting in a vacant field between two houses. As he approached, a door opened in the side of the object and he entered. Inside, he saw a table with maps on it, including one of South America. While he was studying the map, three creatures appeared. They resembled perfectly formed humans but were much smaller. Although they made no move toward him, he found himself backing out of the craft, almost against his will. Once he was outside, the craft took off.

November 8, 1954, Monza, Italy

A huge crowd went to investigate a light and saw three creatures near a disc-shaped object sitting on three legs. The beings spoke with guttural sounds. The creatures got back into their ship, and it lifted without a sound.

November 14, 1954, Isola, Italy

A farmer watched a cigar-shaped object land in a field. When three small beings got out, he was convinced that they were going to steal his rabbits. He ran for his rifle, but when he took aim, it grew so heavy he could not hang on to it. As he dropped it, he became paralyzed. The beings did take the rabbits and returned to their ship. It lifted silently, and when it was gone, the farmer could move again. He picked up his rifle and fired it once at the ship. Apparently he missed.

November 14, 1954, Brazil

A railroad employee spotted three small humanoids who seemed to be examining the railroad bed with a lantern. They wore tight-fitting luminous clothes. When they saw the man, they ran back to their ship, an oval-shaped object, which rose straight into the sky and quickly disappeared.

November 28, 1954, Caracas, Venezuela: Gustave Gonzales and Jose Ponce

Gonzales and Ponce were driving toward a produce warehouse when they sighted a glowing sphere hovering above the street. Gonzales got out and spotted a small, hairy creature with glowing eyes. Gonzales tried to grab the creature which struck him, knocking him backwards. The being then advanced, clawed hands extended, and Gonzales pulled his knife. He struck the creature in the shoulder, but the blade glanced off. Another being came from the ship and both then returned to it. The craft took off swiftly.

December 4, 1954, Pontal, Brazil: José Alves

Alves watched as a disc-shaped object landed and three small men in tight-fitting clothes got out. They gathered samples of the plants, and one took some water from a nearby stream. They then returned to their craft, which took off swiftly.

December 9, 1954, Linha Bela Vista, Brazil

A farmer working in his field heard a sound like a sewing machine and looked up to see a disc-shaped object hovering nearby. The animals in the field under the craft scattered as it landed. Three beings of medium height were visible. One stayed in the craft looking out a hatch while the others walked toward the farmer. The farmer dropped his hoe, and one of the beings picked it up and handed it to him. The alien then uprooted some of the plants. The farmer spoke to the creature, but it didn't seem to understand. Both beings then returned to their craft, and it took off.

December 10, 1954, Caracas, Venezuela

Two men watched two small beings run into the bushes. A few minutes later a glowing disc-shaped object rose into the sky with a sizzling sound.

December 10, 1954, Chico, Venezuela

While hunting, two boys spotted a shiny object they said resembled two soup bowls put together. Four small hairy creatures emerged and tried to drag one of the boys toward the craft. The other boy fired at the creatures with a shotgun, but the buckshot bounced off. The creatures gave up and ran back to their craft. Investigators taken to the site found evidence of a struggle.

December 11, 1954, Linha Bela Vista, Brazil

A farmer went out to investigate a noise and saw an object with a bottom like that of a teakettle, hovering over a field. He saw two humanoids in the field. As the farmer started toward them, they tried to warn him off. When he refused to stop, they pulled up a tobacco plant and ran back to their craft.

December 15, 1954, Campo Grande, Brazil

A fisherman sighted two objects hovering overhead, one revolving around the other. Using the telescopic sight on his rifle, he watched as three creatures descended, gathered samples, and then returned to their craft.

December 16, 1954, San Carlos, Venezuela: Jesus Paz

Three men driving home stopped along the roadside. Jesus Paz got out of the car and walked into the bushes. A moment later he screamed. When his friends ran to his aid, they found him on the ground and saw a short, hairy creature running away. A flat, shiny object then rose into the sky, disappearing in seconds.

December 19, 1954, Valencia, Venezuela

A jockey, running in the cool of the morning, came across a disc-shaped craft hovering just off the ground. Several small creatures were loading boulders into the craft. When they spotted the jockey, they turned some kind of device on him that emitted a purple light that paralyzed him. The creatures returned to their craft and it took off. Later investigations revealed the strange tracks on the ground.

The Wave of 1973

Unlike the earlier UFO-sighting waves, the wave of 1973 included dozens of reports of occupants, abductions, and craft sitting on the ground. When the first "flying discs" were spotted in June 1947, they stayed in the air. By 1973 they were on the ground and hundreds were reporting them.

The first indications of this development came in August, when a man and his son, driving along a New Hampshire highway, saw a tall humanoid standing next to a strange machine in a nearby field. Neither man felt the urge to stop, and they later reported little in the way of additional detail.

In mid-September a Sydney, North Carolina, family reported seeing a creature with glowing red eyes set in the middle of a gray face. The creature, missing a hand, could leap 50 or 60 feet at a time but seemed to limp slightly when not jumping. A search of the field where the creature had been failed to produce any physical evidence.

A radio disc jockey and a group of his friends also reported seeing the creature. They said it had long hair, pointed ears, and a hook nose. They fired five or six shots at it, but didn't say whether they had hit it or if the shots had any effect on it.

A few days later several Savannah, Georgia, teenagers reported seeing ten black dogs run from a landed UFO. Local authorities believed the story to be a hoax.

In October the wave settled in. Reports came from around the country, and nearly every story included a description of an alien creature or a low-flying UFO. On the first day of the month three men reported seeing a huge creature that walked mechanically, like a robot. They also spotted an egg-shaped object. Imprints from landing gear were later found.

On October 4, a Simi Valley, California man, Gary Chopic, spotted a triangular object hovering in a cloud of dust near the Simi Freeway. In a rotating transparent bubble on top of the UFO, Chopic saw a humanoid figure in a silver "wet suit." The creature glanced at Chopic, then leaped from sight, and the bubble began to rotate faster as it disappeared into the object. Chopic heard a whirring sound as a fog seemed to engulf the craft. Seconds later the UFO disappeared. Chopic claimed he didn't see it move; it just vanished. Chopic's report was the second such tale told to Simi Valley authorities.

A retired teacher and her daughter left El Centro, California, the next evening, heading for their home in San Diego. A Greyhound bus and several cars were pulled to the side of the highway. They saw a group of people standing near the side of the road watching a flying disc surrounded by a glistening vapor. As the object climbed to 1,200 feet and disappeared, the vapor seemed to drift down toward the ground. A minute or two later the mist evaporated; none of it reached the ground.

On October 6 a Canadian couple, who requested their names be withheld, watched a bright spotlight bouncing over the ground. They assumed it was the police chasing cattle rustlers. Minutes after they first saw the light, it winked out and they thought nothing more about it. The next morning, however, the woman discovered thick black smoke coming from the area where they had seen the light. She called her husband, and while they were watching the smoke, a "dome-shaped tent" of orange-yellow appeared about a quarter mile away.

A few minutes later a "bulldozer" about a quarter the size of the UFO appeared, heading toward a spring. Five small humanoid "scouts" dressed in bright yellow clothes ran between the two objects. It appeared they wore some sort of helmet, though neither witness was sure.

Neither witness approached the area, but a short time later they noticed that the UFO, the equipment, and the humanoids were gone. They didn't understand how they could have left the area without passing close to the house, but neither went out to inspect the field.

Their daughter, who returned home about noon, went out into the field as soon as she heard the story. She found an area of flattened grass that led from the spot where the UFO had hovered to the small spring. A few days later she discovered more flattened grass and a couple of broken bushes, leading her to conclude that the UFO had returned.

The next occupant report didn't surface until October 11. In Tanner Williams, Alabama, a three-year-old boy told his mother that he had been playing with a nice monster that had wrinkled gray skin and pointed ears. Had it not been for the child's reference to wrinkled gray skin and pointed ears, no one would have remembered the boy's story.

On the same day, October 11, in Connersville, Indiana, just after 4:30 P.M., Terry Eversole and his sister watched a disc-shaped object with a segmented compartment on the bottom hover over a stand of trees. They described the object as silver with a dome on top and three green doors on the bottom. After several seconds it shot off toward the horizon and vanished from sight.

Three hours later, at about 7:30 P.M., Bill Tremper and about fifty others watched an oval object cross the sky above Connersville and hover over a restricted government-owned ammunition testing range. Tremper said the object was pale yellow and had a segmented compartment on the bottom. It settled gently to the ground, was hidden from sight for about thirty minutes, then rose again, hovered again, and disappeared to the northeast.

277

At about 8:00 P.M. that same night, Randi Stevens, Joel Burns, and three others spotted an object hovering near Laurel, Indiana. It looked like two saucers joined at the rim, and its bottom was divided into three equal segments. The UFO hovered for a few minutes, until a truck driver climbed into his cab and blew the horn.

An hour later Charles Hickson and Calvin Parker were fishing from an old pier on the west bank of the Pascagoula River in Pascagoula, Mississippi, when a bright blue light attracted their attention. Within hours, Hickson and Parker were claiming they had been abducted and examined on board the alien craft.

While the press was swarming in Pascagoula, James Cline was awakened by barking dogs in Berea, Tennessee. A farm family saw the blinking lights of a UFO, and Cline saw a creature with a glowing white head cross the road abut 50 feet in front of him. Tracks from both the creature and the UFO were found the next day.

On October 15 a cabdriver on Interstate 90 between Gulfport and Biloxi, Mississippi, reported that his cab had been stalled by a blue UFO that landed in front of him. As he sat staring at the object, he heard a tapping on his windshield and saw a "crablike" claw and two shiny spots. There was speculation that this was the second of the October abductions, but later reports suggest that the cabdriver confessed that he had invented the tale.

On Monday, October 16, William and Donna Hatchett were traveling on an Oklahoma highway when they spotted a bright light to the south. At first William Hatchett thought it was a farm security light on a pole, but it seemed to be coming closer and moving in sync with the truck. When the UFO turned toward them and began descending, Donna Hatchett begged her husband to stop for a moment.

The object hovered near the front of a truck and over a fence line. The couple saw a blinding white light and heard a low-pitched hum. When Donna climbed out of the truck, William, now frightened, warned her to come back. She did so, but got out twice more. When she returned to the truck, Hatchett tried to escape.

The UFO flew off in the opposite direction, gaining altitude but not much speed.

In Drumright, Oklahoma, the Hatchetts reported what they had seen, but they also claimed that they believed the occupants of the UFO had known what they were thinking. The policeman they talked to seemed uninterested in the sighting.

The last sighting on October 16 was reported by two children. The older boy claimed they had seen a UFO with a pointed dome that made a strange buzzing sound. Strange creatures from the craft gave him a chance to look inside, but he was too frightened to do so. The family dog was agitated when the boy's father checked on it just after the UFO left.

The next day was just as busy. In Watauga, Tennessee, a copper-colored UFO hovered just off the ground while a tall creature with clawlike hands and wide blinking eyes reached out to grab two children.

Another tall creature appeared in Falkville, Alabama. Jeff Greenhaw, the police chief, spotted a "being" in a silvery suit and managed to take a photograph of it. Greenhaw had stopped his car when he saw the creature. After a few moments it turned and ran away from him. Greenhaw chased it in his car until he spun off the road.

A cone-shaped UFO piloted by small creatures landed on U.S. Highway 29, southeast of Montgomery, later that day. A car driven by Paul Brown was forced to stop. As Brown got out of his car, two creatures wearing silver suits and white gloves appeared. When they spotted Brown, they returned to their craft and took off. Brown fired several shots from his revolver at the ship.

Another UFO landed on a highway in Mississippi. As one car approached the craft, the car lights went out and the engine died. Occupants of the car spotted a humanoid with a wide mouth, flipper feet, and webbing between the legs.

The third abduction was reported near Loxley, Georgia, on October 17. Clarence Patterson claimed his pickup was sucked into a huge cigar-shaped UFO and that he was jerked free by several robotlike creatures. He blacked out, and when he came to, he was back on the highway driving 90 miles an hour. Few took his report seriously.

The most important case of October 17 came from Utah, where Pat Roach claimed that she was taken from her house by several small creatures. She said the beings came from an object that landed in a field near her home. Roach claimed that she was awakened by her "cat screaming, and I could hear the dog across the street barking." She thought there was a prowler nearby, so she called the police. When they found no prowler and no evidence of a break-in, they left. It would be months before Pat Roach could be convinced that she and some of her children had been abducted.

On October 18 more sightings of UFOs and their crews were reported. Near Chatham, Virginia, two youths reported that they were chased by a white being 3 or 4 feet tall. It had a large head with no eyes, and it ran sideways. Other reports of UFOs in the area made no mention of such a creature.

Also, on October 18, a small silver creature was seen standing by the highway outside Savannah, Georgia. Dozens of cars zipped by but none of them stopped.

That same day, a patrolman for the Noblesville, Indiana, police saw a cigar-shaped object just before midnight. Herchel Fueston had just arrived at the Morse Reservoir when he sighted the UFO in the northeast. When it flew over the reservoir he saw a row of portholes. The UFO hovered briefly, descended to treetop level, and then moved off.

In Copeland, North Carolina, a farm couple discovered an oval-shaped UFO hovering near their home. A small humanoid in a gold jumpsuit was moving near it. The witnesses were afraid of both the craft and the creature, and they didn't approach it.

The last reported sighting of October 18 involved another landed disc. Susan Ramstead said that her car engine stalled as she approached a domed disc sitting in a cornfield near the highway. Using the two-way radio, she called her husband. As she slowed to a stop near the craft, the CB radio ceased working.

The wave didn't slow on October 19. Near Ashland, Georgia, a woman said that her car engine had died and she'd lost her power steering and power brakes. As she coasted to a stop, a small being in metallic clothes appeared. It had a "bubble head" and rectangular eyes. It moved around the car as if inspecting it and then vanished, much to the woman's relief.

Years later, in hypnotic regression, Ramstead remembered the occupants from the landed craft. They were about 5 feet tall, with pasty white faces and large elongated eyes.

She found herself inside a brightly lighted room with machines along one wall. Two aliens were with her. One seemed to watch her while the other touched the machines.

Other aliens entered the room and forced Ramstead to undress. She said that the aliens were male and female. She knew that some of them were women because they had breasts and wore long skirts.

She climbed up onto an examination table and was subjected to the same sort of study that others had reported. She mentioned that her stomach and her knees ached. She said that a cold metal tube entered her body. The aliens took skin and saliva samples. They used hypnosis to probe her mind, and when they finished with the exam, they seemed to lose interest in her.

Left alone, she dressed herself and then waited quietly. Eventually she was escorted back to her car, where she seemed to awaken. The UFO lifted off, and the car engine sputtered to life. The CB radio cleared, and she was able to communicate with her husband. He was panicked, shouting into the radio, but Ramstead convinced him that nothing was wrong. She continued on her way.

The next day, October 20, another abduction took place. This time the woman, Leigh Proctor a college student, vanished for four days. When her car stalled, she pulled to the side of the road. Sitting not far from her was a domed disc. She then spotted three aliens who she claimed had white faces and large eyes on the sides of their heads.

She reported that she was subjected to a wide variety of physical and psychological tests. For long periods she was left alone, but other periods were filled with intense activity. She had no real feel for the passing of time.

When she was released, she walked to the sheriff's office. Although she reported many details of the case, having retained her memory of it, some people didn't believe her story.

On October 21 a mother and her son in Ohio saw a gray humanoid near a landed UFO. A search of the area revealed landing traces.

On October 22 a series of sightings began in nearby Hartford City, Indiana, when Debbie Carney saw two creatures in silver suits cross the road in front of her car. She raced past them and didn't see any sign of a craft.

Fifteen minutes later De Wayne Donathan and his wife saw a flash of light on the road in front of them. At first they believed it was the reflector on the rear of a farm tractor, but as they got closer, they saw two creatures jumping and leaping in a field near the road. Donathan compared the movements to dancing.

Donathan's wife, who was driving, floored the accelerator as she swerved around the creatures. Donathan wasn't sure what they had seen and convinced his wife that they should return. When they did so, they saw nothing but some lights in the distance.

Two hours later Gary Flatter, after hearing the Donathans' story, drove through the area searching for the two creatures. He heard a high-pitched whine and noticed a line of animals running across the road. A moment later he saw the two creatures in the field about 75 feet from him. He turned his truck spotlight on them and was nearly blinded by the reflection from their silver suits. The creatures were about 4 feet tall, had egg-shaped heads, and wore what looked like gas masks with tubes running down to their chests. Shortly after Flatter turned on his light, the creatures leaped out of sight. The next day strange footprints were found in the field.

The wave of sightings declined quickly after that. A couple of reports came from Kentucky, and a man in North Carolina saw a creature with blazing red eyes.

On October 28 the last of the abductions took place. Dionisio Llanca, an Argentine truck driver, checked into a hospital near his home in Bahía Blanca. He claimed that he had pulled over to the side of the road because a tire went flat. As he was changing the tire, the ground around him brightened with a blue glow.

Hovering just off the ground was a domed disc. Standing under the craft were three beings, two male and one female. They were humanoid with long blond hair and elongated eyes. Each wore a one-piece flying-type suit with boots and gloves.

One of the men approached Llanca, and he felt something prick his finger. A feeling of peace spread through him, and he was carried into the craft "on a beam of light." While on the ship, Llanca was subjected to a variety of tests and apparently put into some kind of hypnotic trance.

Three days later Llanca awoke in a vacant field and was taken to the hospital. Examined at length by doctors and including sessions using Pentothol, he revealed the story of his abduction. The doctors, including Eduardo Mata, a psychologist, believed Llanca's story. They found it amazing, but the evidence they saw suggested that it was true.

On November 1 a series of sightings began in New Hampshire when Florence Dow heard a thump on her porch and saw a motionless creature wearing a black coat and a wide-brim hat pulled down over his face, which appeared to be covered with masking tape.

The next night, November 2, Lyndia Morel saw a strange yellow light in the distance as she drove to work. It approached slowly until she could tell that it was a spherical object covered with a honeycomb except for a single oval window. Behind the window she could see the upper body of a creature with wrinkled gray skin and large slanted eyes.

She tried to continue driving to work, but her eyes were drawn to the UFO. Frightened and anxious to get away from it, she pulled into a driveway, leaped from her car, and ran to the door of a farmhouse. She hammered on it, screaming for help, and finally managed to awaken the occupant.

Once inside, she convinced the man that she wasn't crazy, but when he went out to check, the UFO was gone. Morel told the man that she believed the occupant of the craft wanted to capture her.

Two days later Rex Snow and his wife were awakened just after midnight. Outside their house Snow saw two small creatures wearing silver suits. They seemed to be gathering samples of the soil and the vegetation. Snow ordered his German shepherd to attack, but the dog refused to approach the creatures. It ran back into the house. Earlier in the evening, Snow had seen a disc-shaped UFO.

After the series of sightings in New Hampshire, the wave fell off considerably, and only six additional sightings were reported during November and December.

Even a cursory glance at the data for the wave shows that it was different from other periods of UFO activity. Before 1973 there might have been one abduction report a year. Now suddenly there were at least five reported and the suspicion of others. In 1947 the majority of the sightings had involved high-flying discs, in 1952 there had been many radar reports, and in 1957 there was a significant increase in electromagnetic reports. In 1973 there were occupant sightings *and* abduction reports. More importantly, the wide range of descriptions ended with the 1973 wave. A majority of the reports in subsequent years involved small creatures with gray or white faces and large eyes. Certainly there were variations, but those could be explained by the variation in the witnesses, the conditions surrounding the observations, or the variation of the crews.

The descriptions of the UFO crews fall into a basic pattern: humanoids with white faces, elongated eyes, hands that resembled claws, and one-piece flying suits with gloves and boots. The vast majority of occupant reports mention only male crews. During the

1973 wave there were reports of women among the crews—alien females with breasts and long hair, wearing long skirts. Although it could be argued that an alien race wouldn't have women with long hair, this detail was reported by widely scattered witnesses who'd had no opportunity to compare notes.

In some areas the 1973 wave is consistent with sightings from other periods. Betty Hill was the first to mention a needle being inserted in her navel. Now it seemed that every abductee reported a similar experience.

Pat Roach was the first to mention aliens invading her house. Betty and Barney Hill were taken from a car on a deserted stretch of highway. Antonio Villas-Boas was working alone on his farm. Herbert Schirmer was taken from his squad car after he left the road and drove into a field. And in the majority of the 1973 abductions the victims were taken from vehicles in isolated areas. But Roach spoke of them coming into the house, and that seemed to set the trend from that point forward.

Some reports during the 1973 wave also suggested that abduction was the motive. Children reported that aliens tried to grab them, and Lyndia Morel thought the creature in the honeycombed UFO was after her.

The wave of 1973 marked a departure from the norm in this country. There were dozens of landing reports and occupant sightings. Witnesses described aliens who seemed to be gathering samples. In fact, when these reports are examined, one thing becomes clear: this time it seemed that there was a plan behind the wave.

It seems, based on the evidence, that a single group of aliens were operating on Earth for the first time. They came within a limited time frame, starting about the middle of September, worked through October, and were finished by the first week in November. They gathered as much data as they could, grabbing samples and victims quickly. The victims were examined, and the samples and data were apparently stored, to be analyzed at length at a later time.

And that is the one thing that separates the 1973 wave from all the other intense periods of UFO sightings: there was a pattern; the wave seemed to have a scientific purpose. When considered from that point of view, the wave makes some sense. The aliens, whoever they were, had only a short period of time to spend in the vicinity of Earth; they did as much work as they could, and then they got out.

The 1973 Occupant Database

October 1, 1973, Anthony Hill, Tennessee

Three teenagers reported seeing an egg-shaped UFO and a hairy robot that walked with its hands up. Imprints from the landing gear of the craft were later found.

October 4, 1973, Simi Valley, California: Gary Chopic

Chopic saw a triangular object landed near the Simi Freeway. Chopic watched as a humanoid creature crawled around inside a transparent bubble on top. When the occupant spotted Chopic, it scrambled out of sight. The bubble then disappeared into the object as a fog enveloped the craft. A moment later the ship disappeared.

October 6, 1973, Saint Matthias, Quebec, Canada

A man and his wife watched a "dome-shaped tent" hover near a cloud of smoke. Later they saw a small bulldozer and five "scouts" near it wearing bright yellow clothes. After the object, the scouts, and the smoke disappeared, they found an area where the grass had been matted.

October 11, 1973, Pascagoula, Mississippi: Charles Hickson (abduction)

Hickson and Calvin Parker reported that an object hovered near them and that several robotlike creatures exited it. Both men were taken on board the craft and physically examined. After thirty minutes, they were returned to the riverbank.

October 16, 1973, Burbank, California

Two small children reported a buzzing UFO. The beings invited the older boy into the object but the boy was afraid. Minutes after the UFO vanished, the boy's father stepped onto the backyard because the dog was barking.

October 17, 1973, Lehi, Utah: Pat Roach (abduction)

Roach reported seeing occupants from a UFO that landed in a vacant field close to her house. The creatures removed her and four of her children. The youngest reported that some neighbors were also on the craft. The abduction lasted for about thirty minutes.

October 17, 1973, Berea, Tennessee: James Cline

Cline, awakened by barking dogs, spotted a being with a glowing white face about 50 feet away. A nearby farm family saw lights from a UFO in the woods and the next day landing traces were found.

October 17, 1973, Falkville, Alabama: Jeffery Greenhaw (photo)

Greenhaw spotted an alien while investigating a report of a landed UFO. He managed to take a photograph, which many claim shows someone posing in a NASA fire-fighting suit, but this could be the only legitimate photograph of an alien creature. The creature fled down the road with Greenhaw in pursuit. He lost it when his car slid off the road.

October 17, 1973, Danielsville, Georgia: Paul Brown

When a cone-shaped UFO landed on the highway in front of his car, Brown was forced to make a quick stop. Two beings 4 or 5 feet tall appeared under the craft. Brown got out of his car, pistol in hand. The aliens returned to the craft and Brown fired several shots at it without effect.

October 17, 1973, Loxley, Georgia: Clarence Patterson

Patterson claimed that he and his truck were sucked into a huge UFO. He was dragged from his truck by six tall robots that seemed to read his mind. The next thing he knew, he was back on the highway driving 90 miles an hour.

October 18, 1973, Chatham, Virginia

Two youngsters were chased by a 3- to 4-foot-tall being with a shimmering body and a large head that ran sideways. A hazy green cloud was seen drifting away.

October 18, 1973, Savannah, Georgia

A tiny being was seen standing by the highway. Although a number of cars passed it, no one got out of the car.

October 18, 1973: Susan Ramstead (abduction)

After her car stalled as she approached a landed UFO, Ramstead said she saw a number of small aliens. She was taken aboard the craft for a mental and physical examination before being returned to her car.

October 19, 1973, Ashburn, Georgia

A woman's car stalled, and when she pulled to the side of the road, she saw a small metallic man with a bubble-dome head and rectangular eyes. It walked around her car and then disappeared. Afterward she discovered that her engine was billowing smoke and the hood was hot.

October 19, 1973, Copeland, North Carolina

After spotting a blue oval hovering over their home, a farm couple reportedly saw a small humanoid in a gold-colored jumpsuit.

October 20, 1973: Leigh Proctor (abduction—probable hoax)

Proctor, a college student, on her way home, disappeared for four days. When she surfaced, she told a tale of abduction at the hands of several small aliens. Unlike the others abducted during this wave, Proctor was held by the aliens for several days while she was subjected to a battery of tests.

October 21, 1973, Coverdale, Ohio

A mother and son saw a gray humanoid near a landed UFO. The being was surrounded by a bell jar–shaped area of light. Ground traces were found.

October 22, 1973, Hartford City, Indiana: Debbie Carney

Carney saw two small beings in silver suits slowly crossing the road in front of her. As she drove past, they shouted as if trying to scare her.

October 22, 1973, Hartford City, Indiana: De Wayne Donathan

The Donathans saw a pair of beings in bright silver jumping and leaping near the road. Donathan said the beings appeared to be dancing.

October 22, 1973, Hartford City, Indiana: Gary Flatter

Having heard about the sightings, Flatter went out in search of the two beings. After watching a line of small animals running across the road, Flatter spotted the two creatures. When he turned his spotlight on them, they turned to him, their suits reflecting the light. Flatter said the creatures had egg-shaped heads and wore what appeared to be gas masks. The aliens then leaped away. The next day imprints were found in the field.

October 28, 1973, Bahía Blanca, Argentina: Dionisio Llanca (abduction)

Llanca, a truck driver, reported that he saw a glowing blue UFO hovering near him. Three beings, about 5 feet tall in tight-fitting clothes, approached him. He claimed that he was taken on board and given a message to be revealed some time later. He claimed to have been on board the craft for about forty minutes. The authenticity of the case has been seriously questioned.

November 1, 1973, Goffstown, New Hampshire: Florence Dow

After hearing a thump on her porch, Dow saw a figure in an old black coat with a hat pulled down over its eyes. The face was hidden by what appeared to be masking tape.

November 2, 1973, Goffstown, New Hampshire: Lyndia Morel (attempted abduction)

Behind the oval window of a glowing yellow-orange honeycomb-covered UFO, Morel saw a figure with wrinkled grayish skin and large dark egg-shaped eyes. She panicked, fled from her car, and managed to awaken a farmer who let her into his house. When he went out, the UFO was gone.

November 4, 1973, Goffstown, New Hampshire: Rex Snow

Awakened, Snow spotted two small beings in silver suits in his backyard. They had oversize pointed ears, dark egg-shaped eye holes, and large noses. It seemed one held a flashlight while the other gathered samples and put them into a silver bag. Snow had seen a UFO earlier in the evening.

Glossary

AAF. Army Air Force; Army Air Field.

abductee. Someone who claims to have been taken aboard a flying saucer against his or her will and subjected to medical procedures.

AFOSI. Air Force Office of Special Investigation.

APRO. Aerial Phenomena Research Organization (now defunct), started by Coral Lorenzen.

ATIC. Air Technical Intelligence Center.

close encounter. Term coined by Dr. J. Allen Hynek, meaning a close observation of a UFO. A close encounter of the first kind is a close approach to a UFO. A close encounter of the second kind refers to physical traces of the passing of the UFO. A close encounter of the third kind is a sighting of the UFO occupants. A close encounter of the fourth kind (not one of Hynek's original terms) is an abduction.

contactee. Someone who claims to have visited with aliens, ridden in their craft, and been given a message to benefit the human race.

CUFOS. Center for UFO Studies, 2457 West Peterson Avenue, Chicago, IL 60659.

flying saucer. Early term for a UFO. In time it became a derogatory name.

FUFOR. Fund for UFO Research, Box 277, Mount Rainier, MD 20712.

grays. The dark-eyed aliens who are supposedly responsible for the majority of the abductions.

hypnotic regression. A technique in which the subject is placed in a hypnotic state and regressed in time to an event. It is a standard research tool of abduction researchers.

missing time. A period of time about which the subject has no memory although other events surrounding the period are quite clear. Missing time is one of the signposts that suggest abduction.

MUFON. Mutual UFO Network, 103 Oldtowne Road, Seguin, TX 78155.

NICAP. The National Investigations Committee on Aerial Phenomena (now defunct).

Project Blue Book. The official investigation of UFOs by the U.S. Air Force. It ended in 1969.

UFO. An unidentified flying object. The term has become synonymous with "flying saucer" and "extraterrestrial craft," though it simply denotes an object that cannot easily be identified.

Bibliography

Adamski, George. *Inside the Spaceships.* New York: Abelard-Schuman, 1955.

———. *Flying Saucers Farewell.* New York: Abelard-Schuman, 1961.

Asimov, Isaac. *Is Anyone There?* New York: Ace Books, 1967.

ATIC UFO Briefing, April 1952, Project Blue Book Files, National Archives.

"Aurora, Texas, Case, The," *APRO Bulletin,* May-June 1973.

Barker, Gray. "America's Captured Flying Saucers—The Cover-up of the Century," *UFO Report,* May 1977.

———. "Archives Reveal More Crashed Saucers." *Gray Barker's Newsletter,* March 1982.

Bartholomew, Robert E., and Keith Basterfield. "Abduction States of Consciousness," *International UFO Reporter,* March-April 1988.

Binder, Otto. *What We Really Know about Flying Saucers.* Greenwich, Conn.: Fawcett Gold Medal, 1967.

———. *Flying Saucers Are Watching Us.* New York: Tower, 1968.

———. "The Secret Warehouse of UFO Proof." *UFO Report, 1976.*

Bloecher, Ted. *Report on the UFO Wave of 1947.* Washington, D.C.: Self-published, 1967.

Blum, Howard. *Out There: The Government's Secret Quest for Extraterrestrials.* New York: Simon & Schuster, 1991.

Blum, Ralph, with Judy Blum. *Beyond Earth: Man's Contact with UFOs.* New York: Bantam Books, 1974.

Bontempto, Pat. "Incident at Heligoland." *UFO Universe*, Spring 1989.

Bowen, Charles, ed. *The Humanoids*. Chicago: Henry Regency, 1969.

———. *Encounter Cases from Flying Saucer Review*. New York: Signet, 1977.

Brookesmith, Peter. *UFO: The Complete Sightings*. New York: Barnes & Noble, 1995.

Bryan, C. D. B. *Close Encounters of the Fourth Kind: Alien Abduction, UFOs, and the Conference at M.I.T.* New York: Knopf, 1995.

Buckle, Eileen. "Aurora Spaceman—R.I.P.?" *Flying Saucer Review*, July-August 1973.

Bullard, Thomas E. *UFO Abductions: The Measure of a Mystery*. Vol. 1: *Comparative Study of Abduction Reports*. Vol. 2: *Catalogue of Cases*. Mount Rainier, Md.: Fund for UFO Research, 1987.

Cahn, J. P. "The Flying Saucers and the Mysterious Little Men," *True* magazine, September 1952.

———. "Flying Saucer Swindlers." *True* magazine, August 1956.

Canadeo, Anne. *UFOs: The Fact or Fiction Files*. New York: Walker, 1990.

Carey, Thomas J. "The Search for the Archaeologists." *International UFO Reporter*, November-December 1991.

Carpenter, John S. "Gerald Anderson: Truth vs. Fiction." *MUFON UFO Journal*, September 1991.

———. "Gerald Anderson: Disturbing Revelations." *MUFON UFO Journal*, March 1993.

Catoe, Lynn E. *UFOs and Related Subjects: An Annotated Bibliography*. Washington, D.C.: U.S. Government Printing Office, 1969.

Chariton, Wallace O. *The Great Texas Airship Mystery*. Plano, Texas: Wordware, 1991.

Chavarria, Hector. "El Caso Puebla." *OVNI, 1972.*

Clark, Jerome. "The Great Unidentified Airship Scare." *Official UFO*, November 1976.

———. "The Great Crashed Saucer Debate." *UFO Report*, October 1980, 74, 76.

———. "Crashed Saucers—Another View." *Saga's UFO Annual*, 1981.

———. *UFOs in the 1980s*. Detroit: Apogee, 1990.

―――. "Crash Landings." *Omni* magazine, December 1990.

―――. "UFO Reporters. (MJ-12)." *Fate,* December 1990.

―――. "Airships: Part I." *International UFO Reporter,* January-February 1991.

―――. "Airships: Part II." *International UFO Reporter,* March-April 1991.

―――. *The Emergence of a Phenomenon: UFOs from the Beginning Through 1959.* Detroit: Omnigraphics, 1992

―――. *High Strangeness: UFOs from 1960 Through 1979.* Detroit: Omnigraphics, 1996.

Cohen, Daniel, *The Great Airship Mystery: A UFO of the 1890s.* New York: Dodd, Mead, 1981.

―――. *Encyclopedia of the Strange.* New York: Avon, 1987.

―――. *UFOs—The Third Wave.* New York: Evans, 1988.

Creighton, Gordon. "Close Encounters of an Unthinkable and Inadmissible Kind." *Flying Saucer Review,* July-August 1979.

―――. "Further Evidence of Retrievals." *Flying Saucer Review,* January 1980.

―――. "Continuing Evidence of Retrievals of the Third Kind." *Flying Saucer Review,* January-February 1982.

―――. "Top U.S. Scientist Admits Crashed UFOs." *Flying Saucer Review,* October 1985.

Davidson, Leon, ed. *Flying Saucers: An Analysis of Air Force Project Blue Book Special Report No. 14.* Clarksburg, Va.: Saucerian Press, 1971.

Davis, Isabel, and Ted Bloecher. *Close Encounters at Kelly and Others of 1955.* Evanston, Ill.: Center for UFO Studies, 1978.

Davis, Richard. "Results of a Search for Records Concerning the 1947 Crash Near Roswell, New Mexico." Washington, D.C.: U.S. Government Printing Office, 1995.

"The Day a UFO Crashed inside Russia." *UFO Universe,* March 1990.

Dennett, Preston. "Project Redlight: Are We Flying the Saucers Too?" *UFO Universe,* May 1990.

Dobbs, D. L. "Crashed Saucers—The Mystery Continues." *UFO Report,* September 1979.

"DoD News Releases and Fact Sheets," Project Blue Book Files, National Archives, 1952–1968.

Douglas, J. V., and Henry Lee. "The Fireball of December 9, 1965—Part II." *Royal Astronomical Society of Canada Journal* 62, no. 41.

Druffel, Ann, and D. Scott Rogo. *Tujunga Canyon Contacts.* Englewood Cliffs, NJ: Prentice-Hall, 1980.

Edwards, Frank. *Strange World.* New York: Bantam, 1964.

———. *Flying Saucers—Serious Business.* New York: Bantam, 1966.

———. *Flying Saucers—Here and Now!* New York: Bantam, 1968.

Fawcett, Lawrence, and Barry J. Greenwood. *Clear Intent: The Government Cover-up of the UFO Experience.* Englewood Cliffs, N.J.: Prentice-Hall, 1984.

Finney, Ben R., and Eric M. Jones. *Interstellar Migration and the Human Experience.* Berkeley: University of California Press, 1985.

First Status Report, Project STORK (Preliminary to Special Report No. 14), April 1952. Unpublished.

"Flying Saucers." *Look* magazine, 1966 (one-time special issue).

"Flying Saucers Again." *Newsweek,* April 17, 1950.

"Flying Saucers Are Real." *Flying Saucer Review,* January-February 1956.

Foster, Tad. Articles for *Condon Committee Casebook.* 1969. Unpublished.

Fowler, Raymond E. "What about Crashed UFOs?" *Official UFO,* April 1976.

———. *The Andreasson Affair.* Englewood Cliffs, N.J.: Prentice-Hall, 1979.

———. *Casebook of a UFO Investigator.* Englewood Cliffs, N.J.: Prentice-Hall, 1981.

———. *The Andreasson Affair, Phase Two.* Englewood Cliffs, N.J.: Prentice-Hall, 1982.

———. *The Watchers.* New York: Bantam Books, 1990.

———. *The Allagash Abductions.* Tigard, Ore.: Wild Flower Press, 1993.

———. *The Watchers II: Exploring UFOs and the Near Death Experience.* Tigard, Ore.: Wild Flower Press, 1995.

Fry, Daniel W. *The White Sands Incident.* Los Angeles: New Age Publishing, 1954.

Fuller, John G. *The Interrupted Journey.* New York: Dial, 1966.

————. *Incident at Exeter.* New York: Putnam, 1966.

————. *Aliens in the Sky.* New York: Berkley, 1969.

Gillmor, Daniel S., ed. *Scientific Study of Unidentified Flying Objects.* New York: Bantam, 1969.

Goldsmith, Donald. *The Quest for Extraterrestrial Life.* Mill Valley, Calif.: University Science Books, 1980.

————. *Nemesis.* New York: Berkley, 1985.

Good, Timothy. *Above Top Secret.* New York: Morrow, 1988.

————. *The UFO Report.* New York: Avon, 1989.

————. *Alien Contact.* New York: Morrow, 1993.

Gordon, Stan. "The Military UFO Retrieval at Kecksburg, Pennsylvania." *Pursuit* 20, no. 4 (1987).

————. "Kecksburg Crash Update." *MUFON UFO Journal,* September 1989.

————. "Kecksburg Crash Update." *MUFON UFO Journal,* October 1989.

————. "After 25 Years, New Facts on the Kecksburg, Pa. UFO Retrieval Are Revealed." PASU Data Exchange, December 1990.

Hall, Richard. "Crashed Discs—Maybe." *International UFO Reporter.* July-August 1985.

————. *Uninvited Guests.* Santa Fe, N.M.: Aurora Press, 1988.

————, ed. *The UFO Evidence.* Washington, D.C.: NICAP, 1964.

Haugland, Vern. "AF Denies Recovering Portions of 'Saucers.'" *Albuquerque New Mexican,* March 23, 1954.

Hazard, Catherine. "Did the Air Force Hush Up a Flying Saucer Crash?" *Woman's World,* February 27, 1990.

Hegt, William H. "News of Spitzbergen UFO Revealed." *APRG Reporter,* February 1957.

Hopkins, Budd. *Intruders.* New York: Ballantine, 1987.

————. *Missing Time.* New York: Ballantine, 1991.

Huneeus, J. Antonio. "Soviet Scientist Bares Evidence of Two Objects at Tunguska Blast." *New York City Tribune,* November 30, 1989.

————. "Great Soviet UFO Flap of 1989 Centers on Dalnegorsk Crash." *New York City Tribune,* June 14, 1990.

———. "Spacecraft Shot out of South African Sky—Alien Survives." *UFO Universe,* July 1990.

———. "Roswell UFO Crash Update." *UFO Universe,* Winter 1991.

Hynek, J. Allen. *The UFO Experience: A Scientific Inquiry.* Chicago: Henry Regency, 1975.

Hynek, J. Allen, and Jacques Vallee. *The Edge of Reality.* Chicago: Henry Regency, 1972.

"International Reports: Tale of Captured UFO." *UFO* 8, no. 3 (1993).

Jacobs, David M. *The UFO Controversy in America.* New York: Signet, 1975.

———. *Secret Life.* New York: Fireside Books, 1992.

Jones, William E., and Rebecca D. Minshall. "Aztec, New Mexico—A Crash Story Reexamined." *International UFO Reporter,* September-October 1991.

Jung, Carl G. *Flying Saucers: A Modern Myth of Things Seen in the Sky.* New York: Harcourt Brace, 1959.

Keel, John. *Strange Creatures from Space and Time.* New York: Fawcett, 1970.

———. *UFOs: Operation Trojan Horse.* New York: Putnam, 1970.

———. "Now It's No Secret: The Japanese 'Fugo Balloon.'" *UFO* January–February 1991.

———. *The Complete Guide to Mysterious Beings.* New York: Doubleday, 1994.

Keyhoe, Donald E. *Aliens from Space.* New York: Signet, 1974.

Klass, Philip J. *UFOs Explained.* New York: Random House, 1974.

———. *The Public Deceived.* Buffalo, N.Y.: Prometheus, 1983.

———. "Crash of the Crashed Saucer Claim." *Skeptical Enquirer,* Spring 1986.

———. *UFO Abductions: A Dangerous Game.* New York: Prometheus, 1989.

———. "Roswell UFO: Coverups and Credulity." *Skeptical Enquirer,* Fall 1991.

Knaack, Marcelle. *Encyclopedia of U.S. Air Force Aircraft and Missile Systems.* Washington, D.C.: Office of Air Force History, 1988.

Lester, Dave. "Kecksburg's UFO Mystery Unsolved," *Greenburg Tribune-Review,* December 8, 1985.

Lore, Gordon, and Harold H. Deneault. *Mysteries of the Skies: UFOs in Perspective.* Englewood Cliffs, N.J.: Prentice-Hall, 1968.

Lorenzen, Coral and Jim. *Flying Saucers: The Startling Evidence of the Invasion from Outer Space.* New York: Signet, 1966.

———. *Flying Saucer Occupants.* New York: Signet, 1967.

———. *Encounters with UFO Occupants.* New York: Berkley, 1976.

———. *Abducted!* New York: Berkley, 1977.

Mack, John E. *Abduction.* New York: Scribners, 1994.

McClellan, Mike. "The Flying Saucer Crash of 1948 Is a Hoax," *Official UFO,* October 1975.

McDonald, Bill. "Comparing Descriptions, an Illustrated Roswell." *UFO* 8, no. 3 (1993).

McDonough, Thomas R. *The Search for Extraterrestrial Intelligence.* New York: Wiley, 1987.

Menzel, Donald H., and Lyle G. Boyd. *The World of Flying Saucers.* Garden City, N.Y.: Doubleday, 1963.

Menzel, Donald H., and Ernest H. Taves. *The UFO Enigma.* Garden City, N.Y.: Doubleday, 1977.

Michel, Aime. *The Truth about Flying Saucers.* New York: Pyramid 1967.

"Monkeynaut Baker Is Memorialized." Press release. Huntsville, Ala.: Space and Rocket Center, December 4, 1984.

National Security Agency. *Presidential Documents.* Washington, D.C.: Executive Order 12356, 1982.

NICAP. *The UFO Evidence.* Washington, D.C.: NICAP, 1964.

O'Brien, Mike. "New Witness to San Agustin Crash." *MUFON Journal,* March 1991.

Palmer, Raymond, and Kenneth Arnold. *The Coming of the Saucers.* Amherst: 1952.

Papagiannis, Michael D., ed. *The Search for Extraterrestrial Life: Recent Developments.* Boston: 1985.

Peebles, Curtis. *The Moby Dick Project.* Washington, D.C.: Smithsonian Institution Press, 1991.

———. *Watch the Skies.* New York: Berkley, 1995.

Pegues, Etta. *Aurora, Texas: The Town that Might Have Been.* Newark, Texas: Self-published, 1975.

Pritchard, Andrea, David Pritchard, John E. Mack, Pam Casey, and Claudia Yapp, eds. *Alien Discussions: Proceedings of the Abduction Study Conference.* Cambridge, Mass.: North Cambridge, 1994.

"Project Blue Book" (microfilm). National Archives, Washington, D.C.

Prytz, John M. "UFO Crashes." *Flying Saucers,* October 1969.

Quality of the Messenger (film). Crystal Sky Productions, 1993.

Randle, Kevin D. "Mysterious Clues Left Behind by UFOs." *Saga's UFO Annual,* Summer 1972.

————. *The October Scenario.* Iowa City, Iowa: Middle Coast Publishing, 1988.

————. *The UFO Casebook.* New York: Warner, 1989.

————. *A History of UFO Crashes.* New York: Avon, 1995.

Randle, Kevin D., and Robert Charles Cornett. "Project Blue Book Cover-up: Pentagon Suppressed UFO Data." *UFO Report,* Fall 1975.

Randle, Kevin D., and Donald R. Schmitt. *UFO Crash at Roswell.* New York: Avon, 1991.

Randles, Jenny. *The UFO Conspiracy.* New York: Javelin, 1987.

————. *Alien Contacts and Abductions.* New York: Sterling, 1994.

Ring, Kenneth. *The Omega Project: Near Death Experiences, UFO Encounters, and Mind at Large.* New York: Morrow, 1992.

Ruppelt, Edward J. *The Report on Unidentified Flying Objects.* New York: Ace, 1956.

Sagan, Carl, and Thornton Page, eds. *UFOs: Scientific Debate.* New York: Norton, 1974.

Sandreson, Ivan T. "Meteorite-like Object Made a Turn in Cleveland, O. Area." *Omaha World-Herald,* December 15, 1965.

————. "Something Landed in Pennsylvania." *Fate,* March 1966.

————. *Uninvited Visitors.* New York: Cowles, 1967.

————. *Invisible Residents.* New York: World Publishing, 1970.

Saunders, David, and R. Roger Harkins. *UFOs? Yes!* New York: New American Library, 1968.

Scully, Frank. "Scully's Scrapbook." *Variety,* October 12, 1949.

————. *Behind the Flying Saucers.* New York: Henry Holt, 1950.

Slate, B. Ann "The Case of the Crippled Flying Saucer." *Saga,* April 1972.

Smith, Scott. "Q & A: Len Stringfield." *UFO* 6, no. 1 (1991).

"The Space Men at Wright-Patterson." *UFO Update.*

Special Report No. 14, Project Blue Book, 1955.

Spencer, John. *The UFO Encyclopedia.* New York: Avon, 1993.

Spencer, John, and Hilary Evans. *Phenomenon.* New York: Avon, 1988.

Status Reports, "Grudge—Blue Book, Nos. 1–12."

Steiger, Brad. *Strangers from the Skies.* New York: Award, 1966.

———. *Project Blue Book.* New York: Ballantine, 1976.

———. *Alien Meetings.* New York: Ace, 1978

———. *The UFO Abductors.* New York: Berkley, 1988.

Steiger, Brad, and Sherry Hanson Steiger. *The Rainbow Conspiracy.* New York: Pinnacle, 1994

Steinman, William S., and Wendelle C. Stevens. *UFO Crash at Aztec.* Boulder, Colo.: Self-published, 1986.

Stone, Clifford E. *UFOs: Let the Evidence Speak for Itself.* Calif.: Self-published, 1991.

Story, Ronald D. *The Encyclopedia of UFOs.* Garden City, N.Y.: Doubleday, 1980.

Streiber, Whitley. *Communion.* New York: Avon, 1988.

———. *Transformation.* New York: Morrow, 1988.

Stringfield, Leonard H. *Situation Red: The UFO Siege!* Garden City, N.Y.: Doubleday, 1977.

———. *UFO Crash/Retrieval Syndrome: Status Report II.* Seguin, Texas: MUFON, 1980.

———. *UFO Crash/Retrieval: Amassing the Evidence: Status Report III.* Cincinnati, Ohio: Self-published, 1982.

———. "Roswell & the X-15: UFO Basics." *MUFON UFO Journal,* November 1989.

———. *UFO Crash/Retrievals: The Inner Sanctum Status Report VI.* Cincinnati, Ohio: Self-published, 1991.

Sturrock, P. A. "UFOs - A Scientific Debate." *Science* 180 (1973).

Sullivan, Walter. *We Are Not Alone.* New York: Signet, 1966.

Swords, Michael D., ed. *Journal of UFO Studies,* New Series, Vol. 4. Chicago: CUFOS, 1993.

Technical Report, "Unidentified Aerial Objects, Project SIGN," Feb. 1949.

Technical Report, "Unidentified Flying Objects, Project GRUDGE," August 1949.

Templeton, David. "The Uninvited." *Pittsburgh Press*, May 19, 1991.

U.S. Congress, House Committee on Armed Forces. *Unidentified Flying Objects*. Hearings, 89th Congress, 2nd Session, April 5, 1966. Washington, D.C.: U.S. Government Printing Office, 1968.

U.S. Congress Committee on Science and Astronautics. *Symposium on Unidentified Flying Objects*. July 29, 1968, Hearings, Washington, D.C.: U.S. Government Printing Office, 1968.

Vallee, Jacques. *Anatomy of a Phenomenon*. New York: Ace, 1966.

———. *Challenge to Science*. New York: Ace, 1966.

———. *Passport to Magonia*. Chicago: Henry Regency, 1969.

———. *Dimensions*. New York: Ballantine, 1989.

———. *Revelations*. New York: Ballantine, 1991.

"Visitors from Venus." *Time* magazine, January 9, 1950.

Walton, Travis. *The Walton Experience*. New York: Berkley, 1978.

———. *Fire in the Sky*. New York: Marlowe, 1996.

Webb, David. *Year of the Humanoids*. Evanston, Ill.: CUFOS, 1974.

Whiting, Fred. *The Roswell Events*. Mount Rainier, Md.: FUFOR, 1993.

Wilcox, Inez. Personal writings, 1947–1952.

Wilkins, Harold T. *Flying Saucers on the Attack*. New York: Citadel, 1954.

———. *Flying Saucers Uncensored*. New York: Pyramid, 1967.

INDEX